New Essays on
PLATO AND ARISTOTLE

International Library of Philosophy and Scientific Method

EDITOR: A. J. AYER
ASSISTANT EDITOR: BERNARD WILLIAMS

New Essays on
PLATO
and
ARISTOTLE

by

G. E. M. Anscombe Renford Bambrough
G. E. L. Owen J. L. Ackrill
Gilbert Ryle R. M. Hare
Gregory Vlastos D. M. MacKinnon

Edited by
Renford Bambrough

LONDON
ROUTLEDGE & KEGAN PAUL
NEW YORK : THE HUMANITIES PRESS

First published 1965
by Routledge & Kegan Paul Ltd.
Broadway House, 68–74 Carter Lane
London, E.C.4

Printed in Great Britain
by Richard Clay (The Chaucer Press), Ltd.
Bungay, Suffolk

CONTENTS

v

PREFACE

IT is now widely recognised that the study of the history of ancient philosophy can be combined with the first-hand study of philosophical problems and questions, to the advantage of progress in both enquiries. Those who continue to have doubts about the wisdom of such an enterprise can best be answered by presenting actual examples of work in which a serious effort has been made to combine the sympathetic detachment of the scholar with the rigour and circumspection of the philosopher. In so far as a positive and general defence of such attempts can be offered, it has been most forcefully given by Professor Ryle at the end of his celebrated article on "Plato's Parmenides" in *Mind*, 1939:

> There is, of course, always a considerable hazard in attempting to elucidate a doctrine of an earlier philosopher in the light of subsequent and especially of contemporary doctrines. It is always tempting and often easy to read palatable lessons between the lines of some respected but inexplicit Scripture. But the opposite policy of trying to chart the drift of some adolescent theory without reference to the progress of any more adult theories is subject not to the risk but to the certainty of failure. We cannot even state what was a philosopher's puzzle, much less what was the direction or efficacy of his attempt to solve it, unless subsequent reflections have thrown a clearer light upon the matter than he was able to do. Whether a commentator has found such a light or only a will-of-the-wisp is always debatable and often very well worth debating.
>
> Thus I may be wrong in believing that there are affinities between Plato's enquiries in these dialogues and Hume's and Kant's account of assertions of existence, Kant's account of forms of judgement and categories, Russell's doctrine of propositional functions and theory of types, and, perhaps more than any other, nearly the whole of Wittgenstein's *Tractatus Logico-Philosophicus*. I may be wrong in construing these dialogues as, so to speak, forecasting most of the logical embarrassments into which the infinitely courageous and pertinacious Meinong was to fall. But at least my error, if it is one,

does not imply that Plato's puzzles were so factitious or ephemeral that no other serious philosopher has ever experienced any perplexity about them.

These eight essays on Plato and Aristotle were specially written for this volume, and none of them has been published before. The contributors were invited to write on topics in Greek philosophy that were connected with philosophical issues that are still debated by contemporary philosophers, so that their essays would be likely to be of interest both to classical scholars and to philosophers who do not know Greek. Plato and Aristotle loom so large in the history of Greek philosophy, and therefore in the whole history of western philosophy, that it is not surprising that all the contributors chose to write on Platonic and Aristotelian topics, although there are many texts and problems in the pre-Socratic and post-Aristotelian periods which would fall well within the scope of the invitation.

No attempt has been made to enforce any artificial uniformity in the use of Greek words and quotations. Some of the essayists use extensive quotations, and these have been left in Greek type. Others needed only single words or brief phrases, and many of these have been transliterated. The Greekless reader will find that every Greek word or passage that is essential to the understanding of an author's argument has been translated or paraphrased or explained.

The editor gratefully acknowledges the help that he has received from a number of the contributors in the planning and preparation of the book.

RENFORD BAMBROUGH

DEGREES OF REALITY
IN PLATO
Gregory Vlastos

FROM the Greek "is" (ἐστι) we get directly the participle ὄν, the noun, οὐσία, and the adverb, ὄντως. From the English "is" all we can get directly is the participle, *being*, but no noun or adverb. We can't say "beingness" or "beingly", and have to shift to "reality" and "really". But when we do this we lose a verb from the same stem: we can't say, "Socrates reals a man" or "Socrates reals wise", unless we want to start one of those overstrenuous linguistic games, like Hegelese or Heideggerese. If we want to talk English, we will have to break up the consanguineous Greek quartet into two etymologically unrelated groups, picking our verbs from the first, our noun and adverb (and also the exceptionally useful adjective, "real") from the second. This is no great hardship. But it makes less than obvious what leaps to the eye in the Greek: that "real" and "reality" are simply the adjectival and nominal forms of "to be", and that "is" in turn represents the verbal form of "real" and "reality".

Plato does not speak of "grades" or "degrees" of reality. He says such things as these: The Form is "completely" real,[1] or "purely" real,[2] or "perfectly" real,[3] or "really" real,[4] it is "more

[1] παντελῶς ὄν *Rep.* 477a.

[2] τοῦ εἰλικρινῶς ὄντος, *Rep.* 477a, 478d, 479d. Cf. the allied use of εἰλικρινές (followed by καθαρόν, ἄμεικτον) in *Symp.* 211e. Here it is used as a modifier not of ὄν, but of a specific Form, αὐτὸ τὸ καλόν in order to contrast that Form with its instances. And cf. p. 5, n. 3, and p. 6, n. 2.

[3] τελέως ὄν, *Rep.* 597a.

[4] κλίνης ὄντως οὔσης: the Form, Bed, *Rep.* 597d. Cf. τὸ ὂν ὄντως (*Phil.* 59d) and

real"[1] than its sensible instances, which are said to "fall between the purely real and the wholly unreal" (477a), because their state is such that "they both are and are not" (477a–478d). I want to ask three questions: First, what is the sense of "real" and "reality" in these statements? Second, why does Plato think the Forms are "more real" in this sense than are their sensible instances?[2] Third, what are the philosophical merits and demerits of this doctrine?

I

"True" is a fairly common meaning of "real" in spoken and written Greek. Thus Plato will say, "to speak (or, think) the real" for "to speak (or, think) the truth".[3] Moreover, in Greek, as in English, the predicate, "true", applying primarily to propositions, may also apply, derivatively, to things described by propositions —to objects, persons, stuffs, states, processes, dispositions, and the like.[4] In either language one can speak of "a true friend", "true gold", "true courage", and so forth. In all such cases "real"

[1] μᾶλλον ὄντα Rep. 515d. This is said of the figurines in the Cave which are to their shadows on the wall as are the Forms to their sensible instances. In Rep. 585d the soul, nourished ("filled") by the Forms, is said to be τὸ τῶν μᾶλλον ὄντων πληρούμενον.

[2] I regret that limitations of space make it impossible for me to deal here with other recent discussions, some of which would not even agree with my way of posing the question: W. F. R. Hardie, A Study in Plato, Oxford, 1936, pp. 27 ff.; J. Moreau, La Construction de l'Idealisme Platonicien, Paris, 1939, Chap. 7; the symposium by G. Brown, G. C. Field, and S. S. Orr in Proc. Arist. Soc., Suppl. Vol. 19 (1945), pp. 169 ff.; G. C. Field, The Philosophy of Plato, Oxford, 1949, Chaps. 2 and 3; N. R. Murphy, The Interpretation of Plato's Republic, Oxford, 1951, Chap. 6, and pp. 197 ff. in Chap. 9; W. Bröcker, "Platons ontologischer Komparativ", Hermes 87 (1959), pp. 415 ff.; J. Gosling, "Rep. V: τὰ πολλὰ καλά, etc.", Phronesis 5 (1960), pp. 116 ff.; R. E. Allen, "The Argument from Opposites in Republic V", Review of Metaphysics 15, 1961, pp. 325 ff. But my greatest debt is to Mr. G. E. L. Owen, whose views on this topic I came to know from one of his unpublished MSS, and from discussion with him in Oxford in 1960.

[3] E.g. Rep. 389c: the expressions τὰ ὄντα λέγειν, τἀληθῆ λέγειν, are used synonymously. Cf. Tht. 179c, 199a.

[4] For the Greek see Greek–English Lexicon, Liddell and Scott, Revised edition by H. S. Jones (hereafter "LSJ"), s.v. ἀληθής II; ἀληθινός, I (2).

οὐσία ὄντως οὖσα (Phdr. 247c) of the Forms. The world of becoming is ὄντως οὐδέποτε ὄν, Tm 28a.

2

can be substituted for "true" with little change of sense. We speak of "a real friend", "real gold", and the like. When we do this we think of things or persons as having those very properties in virtue of which they can be truly so described: e.g. of Jones as sympathetic, responsive, considerate, loyal, and whatever else we expect of a man whom we would call "a friend" when weighing our words, using them strictly and with a full view of the facts. Grammar itself would make this obvious if we had in English, as in Greek, a copula which is a verbal cognate of "real". For we would then be saying that Jones is a "real" friend because he "reals" (= is) *sympathetic, responsive,* etc.; i.e. because he has those attributes in virtue of which sentences applying these predicates to him are true and would be found to be true if put to the test. This implicit reference to reliable truth is all that saves "real" from redundancy when used in this sense. There would be no point in saying that Jones is a "real" friend, as distinct from just saying that he is a friend, unless we were tacitly contrasting him with people who talk and act like friends, and for a time pass for friends, but then turn out to be fakes, i.e. unless we were expressing the conviction that Jones has "proved" a friend, or would "prove" one under trial.[1]

What of "more real"? We would have no use for this expression if the logic of all predicates were like that of "diamond", which divides all possible candidates for the description into just two classes, those which are ("real") diamonds, and those which are not, with no intermediate category in between: the finest imitation diamond in the Fifth Avenue jewellery shop is no more of a real diamond than is the cheapest fake in Woolworth's. But in a wide variety of predicates we do want to recognise intermediate cases between the "real" and "not real" thing of that kind. A man may not be all one expects from a *friend* or from a *scientist* or a *poet,* yet measure up so much better to these descriptions than would any number of others that we would have no hesitation in saying that he is more of a real friend,[2] or scientist, or poet,

---

[1] X "proving *himself*" an F, when what is "proved" is a set of propositions asserting him to be an F, parallels the linguistic manoeuvre which allows us to say that he is a "true" F, when what we mean is that the relevant propositions are true.

[2] "A more real friend" would not be possible English. I cannot think of any unstrained example of "*x* is a more real F than is *y*" in common speech.

than they. Or, to take a very different case: We see a painting, executed only partly by Rubens, the rest of the work done by pupils in his studio. Is this a "real" Rubens? It is, and it is not. It is more of one, certainly, than is an outright fake. But it is much less of one than would be a Rubens whose every brush-stroke came from the master's hand. The latter—the "real Rubens"— is what we would use as our authoritative source of knowledge of what "a Rubens" is.

When we try out this sense of "real" and "more real" in Plato we find uses that approach it closely. A fine example is his first use of "more real": $\mu\hat{a}\lambda\lambda\rho\nu$ $\check{o}\nu\tau a$[1] in *Republic* 515d. The passage is in the Allegory of the Cave. The man who had lived facing away from the light has just turned around to catch with dazzled eyes his first uncertain glimpse of the figures on the parapet that cast the shadows he had been taking for the "real" things his whole life long:

> What do you suppose would be his answer if we were to tell him that he had seen nothing but trash heretofore, but that now, because he is[2] somewhat closer to reality and has turned towards more real things, he sees more correctly? And if we were to point to each of these passing objects [the figures] and make him answer the question, "What is it?", don't you suppose he would be puzzled and count the things he had been seeing heretofore more true ($\dot{a}\lambda\eta\theta\dot{\epsilon}\sigma$-$\tau\epsilon\rho a$) than the ones pointed out to him now? (515d)

Suppose it were the statuette of a horse that he is looking at just now. In the most obvious sense of "real" this is no more of a "real horse" than are its silhouettes: no more than they is it a horse one needs to feed, can ride to town, and the like. But this sense of "real" has been screened out in the Allegory. Chained to his place, immobilised totally (he cannot even move his head), he has been drained of every mundane interest. The only thing left for him to be is *homo cognoscens*. The things he calls "horses" he scans with pure intellectual curiosity, intent on one thing only: to find out what he can, just by looking, in answer to the "What is it?"[3]

---

[1] The first occurrence of $\mu\hat{a}\lambda\lambda\rho\nu$ with a participle of the verb *to be* in surviving Greek philosophical prose.

[2] The copula, not in the text, "is easily supplied" (Adam *ad loc.*).

[3] The question which continues to epitomise the quest for knowledge in the *Phaedo* (75d, 78d) and the *Republic* (490d, 532ab, 533b) as it did in the earlier Socratic dialogues.

4

question. It is for just this purpose that he is now "somewhat closer to reality and has turned towards more real things": looking at the figure of a horse before him "he sees more correctly" what a horse is.[1] The man who made it, let us suppose, was a fine craftsman, like one of those who cut the frieze of the Parthenon; his art-work is a boon to the mind as much as to the eye, a store-house of anatomically true information about the structure of a horse's body.[2] It will be a revelation to our prisoner once he gets used to the light and learns how to read three-dimensional signs. Thus this "horse" is "more real" than its shadows in the very same sense in which it is "more true" and "more clear":[3] it yields a better disclosure of what a horse is. Even so, it is not nearly as adequate for this purpose as the horse he will encounter when he climbs out of the Cave into the world above—the model from which the craftsman got his knowledge of horses, the most authoritative source the visible world can offer of true answers to the question, "What is a horse?" This is what symbolises in the Allegory "the F itself",[4] the Form.

This is the sense in which the Form of the Bed in *Rep.* X (597a, d) is the "really real" or "perfectly real" Bed. This we would know even if we had not been given earlier the Cave to tell us how to take these startling expressions. Plato explains himself all over again here, saying that the bed-maker's product is "something dark (ἀμυδρόν τι) by comparison with the truth (πρὸς ἀλήθειαν), i.e. by comparison with the 'true' Bed)"—"dark" to the mind when

---

[1] The logical connection between the "more real" and that which enables one to "see more correctly" is built into the construction of Plato's sentence. The full sense I take to be: because the figure is more of a real F than the shadow, one sees more correctly the nature of F when looking at ("turned towards") the figure.

[2] All this only as an aid to the exposition. Without blowing up the Allegory in this way we could still count on a figure that yields *some* knowledge in excess of what can be got out of its shadows. So much even a third-rate artist would put into his horse.

[3] For "true" see, in addition to ἀληθέστερα at 511d 6 (paralleling μᾶλλον ὄντα at d 3), τὸ ἀληθές at 515c 2, and the analogous use of ἀληθῶν at 516a 3. Σαφέστερα at 515e 4 parallels ἀληθέστερα just before; both are carry-overs from the Line: the "truer" the objects, the "clearer" their apprehension, 509d–510a and 511e.

[4] Cf. αὐτὰ τὰ ζῷα, αὐτὰ ἄστρα, αὐτὸν τὸν ἥλιον, 532a 3–5, where the relative pronoun is a forceful reminder of one of the standard expressions for the Forms which had been used not long before our passage (507b, αὐτὸ καλόν, αὐτὸ ἀγαθόν).

5

it seeks light on the question, "What are those properties which make up the essence of *Bed*?"[1] The same point is made by another tale, the one compressed into the word "pure" as applied to the Forms already in the *Phaedo*,[2] then used again in the *Symposium*, and occurring three times in adverbial form in *Rep.* V as a variant for the "perfectly" or "completely" real.[3] As is clear in this latter passage—the first and also the fullest exposition of degrees of reality—the intended contrast is between the Form, *F*, and instances of it which are reckoned less "pure" *F*'s than it, because they are not exclusively *F*, but are *F* and not-*F*:[4] their *F* nature is adulterated by contrary characters, so that we could only get a confused[5] and uncertain idea of what it is to be *F*, one that would be subject to constant fluctuations[6] as we encountered

---

[1] The Form *per contra* is σαφές (cf. p. 5, n. 3), the opposite of ἀμυδρόν (cf. *Soph.* 250e). The lucidity of the Form—its cognitive visibility, as it were—was already brought out in the Simile of the Sun: the intelligible world is the one "where truth and reality shine forth (καταλάμπει)", while the sensible world is "mixed with darkness" (508d). The same imagery in the Cave, especially at 518c: the release from the Cave is a "turning from darkness to the light" and reaches, at its height, "the brightest of realities (τοῦ ὄντος τὸ φανότατον)," the Form of the Good.

[2] When freed from the body we shall come to know "all of them (*sc.* the Forms) in their purity (αὐτῶν πᾶν τὸ εἰλικρινές), which is, I take it, the truth (τὸ ἀληθές)," 67b; cf. 66a. Καθαρόν is also used to the same effect (*Phdo* 67b; *Symp.* 211e; *Rep.* 585b; *Phil.* 59c); so too ἄμεικτον (*Symp.* 211e, *Phil.* 59c) and μονοειδές (*Phdo* 78d, *Symp.* 211b, e).

[3] See p. 1, n. 2.

[4] The warrant for expanding the "is and is not" of 477a–479d into "is and is not *F*" is 479c 3–4 taken in conjunction with 479b 9–10: "Then *is* each of the many, rather than *is not*, whatever one asserts that it is (*sc.* big or small, heavy or light, etc.)?" This shows what has to be supplied when the "is and is not" formula is used without this supplement (e.g. immediately after, at c 4; or, by the same token, in the earlier occurrences of the formula, 477a, 478de).

[5] Cf. *Phil.* 53ab: the "truest" white is the "purest" (τὸ μάλιστ' εἰλικρινές), the one least adulterated by admixture (ἀκρατέστατον) with any other colour. Cf. also *Rep.* 523c ff.: the reason why sight and the other senses are defective in their disclosures (ἐνδεῶς δηλοῦσιν 523e) of such things as largeness, smallness, thickness, thinness, softness, hardness, etc. (523e) is that, in their sensible presentations, each of these is "confused" with its opposite: for "clearness" (σαφήνεια) in their apprehension we must resort to νόησις which is able to see them "not confused but distinguished" (οὐ συγκεχυμένα ἀλλὰ διωρισμένα) or "separated out" (κεχωρισμένον), 524c.

[6] κυλινδεῖται, 479d 4; ἐν πολλοῖς καὶ παντοίως ἴσχουσιν πλανώμενοι, 484b 6.

6

instances of F that turned out to be different in one or more respects from those on which we based our previous conception of it.

Here, then, is one sense of "real": that which is cognitively dependable, undeceiving. And since this will give me more than enough to explore in this paper, I shall be content to work with this alone, and shall accordingly speak of it for convenience as "the" sense of "real" for Plato. But I am not suggesting that this is the only sense of "real" for him.[1] On the contrary, I am certain that he crosses this sense with a very different one which becomes most prominent when he thinks of the "really real" things, the Forms, as objects of mystical experience.[2] This calls for a separate investigation, whose results I cannot anticipate here, except to say that in this other sense of "real" the word functions as a value-predicate,[3] but one that transcends the usual specifications of value, moral, aesthetic, and religious; it connotes more than goodness, beauty, or holiness, or even than all three of them in conjunction. I will do nothing to placate those readers who will be outraged at the suggestion that Plato should use "real" in his degrees-of-reality doctrine in two senses as different as these. All I can say to them is that I am only reporting the facts as I see them; and that the facts of Plato's usage compel me to recognise the occurrence of the word in this other sense which differs demonstrably from that of "cognitively reliable". For example: while all Forms are "real" in the cognitive sense, not all could be "real" in the evaluative sense: not the Forms, Injustice, Ugliness,

---

[1] This disclaimer has important consequences for the interpretation of "the" degrees-of-reality theory offered in sections II and III below. The fact is that Plato has in effect *two* (overlapping) theories, the second being a construct on the second sense of "real" which I shall mention directly. This second theory I *ignore completely* in this paper. I could not even begin to explain it properly within my space-budget.

[2] As e.g. at *Rep.* 490b, 500c; *Phdr.* 247c ff.

[3] So far as things fail to be real they are "trash" (cf. φλυαρίας, *Rep.* 515d) unworthy of "serious concern" (σπουδάζειν), *Rep.* 599ab. For the connection between worthlessness and not-being note the common use of οὐδενία (literally, "nothingness") to *mean* worthlessness (twice in untechnical contexts in Plato: *Phdr.* 235a, τῆς ἐμῆς οὐδενίας, *Tht.* 176c, οὐδενία τε καὶ ἀνανδρία.) (For this use of "being" by the mystics, cf. Meister Eckhart: "a stone, to the extent that it has being, would be better than even God and the Godhead without being", R. B. Blakeney, *Meister Eckhart, a Modern Translation*, New York, 1941, p. 172).

Evil, for instance.[1] These are mentioned as bona fide Forms on a level with Justice, Beauty, and Goodness. Cognitively they must be on a par with the rest, members in good standing of that highest realm of intelligible Being which is made up of all, and only, Forms. Yet obviously it is not of such Forms as these that Plato thinks when he speaks of the vision of Form as "the most blessed of all mystic initiations",[2] and of the Forms themselves as "unblemished, whole, tremorless, blessed apparitions" (*Phdr.* 250c), divine, and more so than traditional gods.[3] Plato's thought at this point is not wholly free from an incoherence[4] which we could only smooth out of the record by misrepresenting our data. But this is not the place to pursue this theme. I mention it only to warn the reader of complications I am wilfully ignoring in order to concentrate on the questions that bear more directly on the cognitive sense of "real" to which I am devoting this paper.

What of that other sense of ἔστι and its derivatives—the one we convey by "exists" in English?[5] As we commonly use the word "existence",[6] degrees of it (as distinct from degrees of perfection of things in existence) make no sense whatever; the idea of one

---

[1] Cited without hesitations or apologies at *Rep.* 475e, 476.

[2] *Phdr.* 250bc. Cf. *Phdo* 69cd.

[3] By implication at *Phdr.* 249c 6 (Burnet's text).

[4] Though mitigated by the fact that the bad Forms would still be good from one point of view: they would satisfy the cognitive interest.

[5] I cannot go here into the difficult question of whether or not Plato ever formally distinguished the existential from the predicative uses of "is". But it may be worth pointing out that in contexts where his need to express existence in our common use of the term (see next note) is most urgent he tends to eke out "to be" with locatives: "it makes no difference whether it (the Ideal State) exists *somewhere* or will exist (εἴτε που ἔστιν εἴτε ἔσται)", *Rep.* 592b; we should not fear that the soul may be dissipated at death, "vanishing into thin air and existing *nowhere*" (καὶ οὐδὲν ἔτι οὐδαμοῦ ἔστι, *Phdo* 84b, Hackforth's translation).

[6] I.e. applying it to individuals: God, crocodiles, unicorns, etc. I say this to exclude the (much rarer) cases where we apply "existence" to general terms—"justice", "opportunity", "clear thinking", and so forth—to signify not their abstract, "platonic", existence, but their concrete instantiation; in *this* use of "existence" provision for degrees of it is normal: if I were to list the countries in which "justice exists" I might well be expected to admit that it exists in higher degree in some than in others. But this is only another way of referring to degrees of perfection: "*F* exists in higher degree at *a* than at *b*" = "*F* is more completely realised at *a* than at *b*"; so we would be back to degrees of reality in the sense discussed above.

individual existing more, or less, than another would be a rank absurdity. It would take strong, unambiguous evidence to establish that Plato had any such thought in mind when he spoke of some things as being more, or less, real than others. And there is no such evidence. Would anyone seriously suggest that Plato wants to undermine our faith in the existence of the beds we sleep on, buy and sell, etc., when he compares their "being" unfavourably with that of their Form in *Rep.* X?[1] His contention that they are not "really real" surely *presupposes* their existence. Similarly the sight-lovers in *Rep.* V are not told that the faces, bodies, spectacles, etc.,[2] they love to see do not exist or only half exist (whatever that might mean): they are mistaken about the reality of the beauty—not of the existence—of the things of sense. The dream-metaphor both here (476cd) and elsewhere (*Tm* 52bc) should not be misunderstood: It could not be implying or alluding to degrees of existence, even if its point were that sensible things are mental images; for Plato would then be telling us not that they half exist, but that they do not exist and are only illusions of mortal mind. But Plato, of course, is no Parmenides: the sensible world is the *object*, not the creature, of *doxa*. He uses the dream-metaphor to liken the state of mind of the philosophically unenlightened to that of the dreamer in only one respect: both are systematically deceived in taking things which are not really (or truly) F for the real (and true) F.[3] Their mistake is not to take half existents for full existents, but deceitful resemblances of F for the real F.

---

[1] Cf. N. R. Murphy, *op. cit.*, p. 128: "Book X is able to treat the beds made by carpenters as 'incompletely real' without casting any slur on the physical existence of what the carpenter put together." But Murphy's next step is to deny altogether the applicability of degrees of reality to the physical world. He would explain Plato's clear-cut statements to the contrary as follows: "The general rule on which he is working seems clear enough. Whenever we speak of an unreality it is not with reference to false things but to false thoughts. 'Unreal' applies only to the objects of false thinking or unfounded suggestion of some kind. It is predicable of what would be real if a false thought were true," *ibid.*, p. 129. But nothing can be more certain than that Plato considers the physical world itself less real than the Forms, and thinks he can *thereby* account for our incapacity to reach adequately true thoughts of it (*Rep.* 477–9; *Tm* 28–9).

[2] For the interpretation of πολλὰ τὰ καλά in this passage see p. 11, n. 2.

[3] This is explicit at *Rep.* 476cd, implicit at *Tm* 52bc.

II

I may now tackle my next question: *Why* does Plato think the Forms cognitively "more real" than their sensible instances? His own answer to this question in *Republic* V is as direct and emphatic as it is cryptic: because, he says, the sensibles are always, the Forms never, *F* and not-*F*.[1] All he then does to explain this claim is to go down the line with a number of substitutions for *F*—beautiful, just, pious, double, large, heavy—and simply *assert* that each of the "many beautifuls" is also not beautiful, and so forth. But why this should be so, he does not say. He must be assuming that the point he is making is so familiar to his audience that it calls for no special exposition or argument at this time. In such circumstances all we can do is to thumb his works for some passage which speaks more informatively on this point. The best one by far for this purpose is *Symp.* 211a: That "wonderful sort of Beauty" the lover will see at the height of his ascent, will not be

(1) beautiful in one respect, ugly in another,[2] nor yet

(2) beautiful at one time, but not at another, nor yet

(3) beautiful in relation to some things, ugly in relation to others, nor

(4) beautiful here, ugly elsewhere, being beautiful for some, ugly for others.

Here, laid out for our inspection, are four grounds on one or more of which the "*F* and not-*F*" formula can be clamped on any sensible instance of Beauty:

(1) It may be beautiful in one of its features, ugly in another, as a vase might have an exquisite shape, but garish colours.[3]

(2) It may be beautiful at one time, not at a later one,[4] as a flower, lovely in the bud, might be coarse and shapeless at full bloom.

(3) It may be beautiful by comparison with one thing, ugly by

[1] 479a–d. Cf. p. 6, n. 4.

[2] For the sense of the τῇ ("there", "on that spot", "in that way") see LSJ, *s.v.* ὁ, A. VIII. 1.

[3] And/or beautiful in one of its parts, ugly in another (say, flower and leaves respectively).

[4] The point to which Plato alludes when he says that the sensibles are scarcely ever, the Forms invariably, "in the same state": e.g. *Phdo* 78d–79e, 80b; *Rep.* 479a, 484b, 530b; *Phil.* 59c. Cf. *Crat.* 439d; *Tm* 49e.

comparison with another, as the beautiful girl in the *Hippias Major* is said to be ugly by comparison with a goddess.[1]

(4) It may be beautiful in one spatial location, ugly in another, as a painting meant to be seen from a certain distance might appear beautiful if properly placed, ugly if crowded into a small room.[2]

A host of questions raised by each of these four grounds must be suppressed to concentrate on just one: Why should Plato think that a thing judged *F* and not-*F* on any of these grounds "less real" than the corresponding Form? I find the best clue to the answer in a passage in the *Phaedo* (102bc): After telling us that Simmias is both *F* and not-*F* (tall and short) on the third of the above grounds (he is taller than Socrates and shorter than Phaedo), Plato remarks that

of course, you will admit that the truth of the matter is not expressed by the words, "Simmias is taller than Socrates." For surely it is not in Simmias' nature that he should be taller than Socrates because he

---

[1] 289d: on this account she is "no more beautiful than ugly", 289c; cf. *Rep.* 479b 9–10. On the same ground the finger will appear both large and small, thick and thin, soft and hard, at *Rep.* 523e.

[2] I have expounded the "*x* is *F* and not-*F*" formula for the cases in which the *x* would be an individual. This is what Plato usually has in view when thinking of sensible instantiations of Forms, as e.g. in the girl and finger examples above, and frequently elsewhere: the visibles in the Line are "the living creatures about us, and all things that grow naturally, and all man-made objects", *Rep.* 510c; the ἕκαστα τὰ πολλά are illustrated by tables and beds in *Rep.* 596a 6–7; the "many beautifuls" by "men, horses, garments" in *Phdo* 78d, and instances of beauty, in contrast to the Form, by "a beautiful face" in *Crat.* 439d; the many similars by "you and me" in *Parm.* 129a. But (*a*) actions or, more generally, occurrences, and (*b*) usages or institutions would also count for Plato as sensible instances of Forms. Thus he is obviously thinking of (*a*) when he cites "sounds" (along with "colours and shapes and everything fashioned from such things") at *Rep.* 476b (cf. 480a), and of both (*a*) and (*b*) when he speaks at 479a (cf. also 479e) of the many δίκαια and ὅσια, each of which will also appear as the contrary of just or pious. The above four grounds on which an individual can be *F* and not-*F* would apply just as well to actions and usages, provided only we take account of the fact that the criterion of identity would be suitably different: the *same* action or usage would be one which answers to the same description, even if performed by different individuals. Thus it is on the assumption that "burying one's ancestors" would be the same action whether performed by Tantalus, Dardanus, Zethos, or Pelops (*Hp Maj.* 293b) that it is shown to be τοῖς μὲν ... καλόν, τοῖς δ' οὐ καλόν, 293c. For a different interpretation of "the many" Fs of *Rep.* V see Murphy, *op. cit.*, pp. 106 ff., and Gosling, *op. cit.*, pp. 116 ff.

is Simmias (τῷ Σιμμίαν εἶναι),[1] but rather because of the height he happens to have.

Here that *Simmias is taller than Socrates* (call this "S1") is a true proposition. Why then does it not "express the truth of the matter?" What sort of "truth" is it that S1, though true, does not succeed in expressing? The kind we would reach if we turned instead, for example, to one of the propositions that come into the discussion a little later (104A):

(S2) Three is odd.

Now S2 differs from S1 in that radical way whose vast importance for the theory of knowledge Plato was the first to recognise in the history of Western thought. One way of putting this would be to say that S2 takes us out of the domain of contingent truth, which is all we can get out of S1, into that of logical necessity. This particular phraseology would not, of course, be Plato's. But he would be telling us much the same thing in his own language if he said that while S1 and S2 are both true, S1 can only be a true belief, while S2 constitutes knowledge—"knowledge" in his own ultra-strong sense of the word, which he first broached in the *Meno* (98a) when he said that a true belief becomes knowledge when it has been "bound" or "tied" by "calculation of the reason",[2] implying that the required "binding" or "tying" is that which connects statement with statement by logical inference or term with term by logical analysis. When a belief gets this kind of "binding" it is no longer *fallible* in the importantly relevant sense, i.e. capable of being proved false by refinements and extensions of the very process which gave us reason to think it true in the first place. It has now become "infallible", or "unshakeable".[3] This is strong language, but it is Plato's. It conveys the sense of complete security he gets from statements which come up to his standards for knowledge—those whose truth-claims owe nothing to sensory observation and everything to logical inference and analysis.

[1] For the significance of this construction see the passages compared with τῷ μελίττας εἶναι by E. S. Thompson (*Plato's Meno*, London, 1901), *ad Meno* 72b.

[2] *Αἰτία* in *αἰτίας λογισμῷ* should not be translated "cause" (the Jowett rendering, reappearing in the most recent commentary, *Plato's Meno*, R. S. Bluck, Cambridge, 1961, *ad loc.*), but as "the because" or "the reason" (the latter in W. K. C. Guthrie's translation, *Plato's Protagoras and Meno*, London, 1956.) *Αἰτία*, as used by Plato and Aristotle, *need* not connote causal agency.

[3] ἀναμάρτητον, *Rep.* 477e; ἀμεταπτώτους, *Tm* 29b.

Now since Plato habitually thinks of knowledge as a relation between the mind and its objects, he would naturally transpose what I have said for him from properties of statements expressing knowledge to properties of objects known. These are, of course, the Forms. So to have the requisite internal binding, a statement of the form "F is H" would have to be about the Forms, F and H, and be true because these characters are logically or essentially connected. The reason why F is H would then be discernible in the very "nature" of F, in its "what it *is*",[1] its "isness" as Shorey once jokingly converted the Greek into impossibly literal English; or, in possible English, its *reality*. Here, Plato would assure us, we would have found our way to something completely reliable, and hence completely "real" in the sense I have explained. For whatever statements about F follow from the logical analysis of this character (and/or the analysis of characters to which F is logically related) would be *necessary* statements, hence, in Plato's language, "infallible" ones—statements which could never go wrong. Contrariwise, any statements we make about a sensible instance of F would be fallible precisely because the sensible instance does not admit of such necessary connection with its predicates. When a particular, a, is F, you can't say that a is F because of *being a*: It is not because of his *being* Simmias that Simmias is taller than Socrates; there is no such thing as *being a* (*being Simmias*, unlike *being tall*, or *being human*, is not a character).[2] Hence there is nothing to which the character F can be tied in such a way that it would follow "infallibly" that a is F. So the "a is F" predication will be loose and shaky, and you should not be surprised to find the contrary of F, or of any other character you may ascribe to a, also turning up in one or more of three ways answering to the first, second, and fourth of the four grounds enumerated above:

(1) Since a will then have various features—say, its colour, smell, taste, texture, weight, shape—belonging to it by empirical conjunction, not by logical connection, a may very well be F in respect of one of them, not-F in respect of one or more

[1] The ὅ ἐστιν (or οὐσία) which answers the τί ἐστιν question of note 3, on p. 4.
[2] Cf. R. G. Turnbull, "Aristotle's Debt to the 'Natural Philosophy' of the *Phaedo*," *Philosophical Quarterly 8* (1958), pp. 131 ff., at pp. 132, 140, 141.

others.[1] Then *a* will be *F* and not-*F* on the first ground: in different respects.

(2) Since *a* is a temporal thing, and there is no logical connection between every property it has at time 1 and every property it has at time 2, it may happen that *a* is *F* at time 1 and not-*F* at time 2. So *a* will be *F* and not-*F* on the second ground: at different times.

(4) Since *a* is a spatial object, and there is no logical connection between the characters it has, or appears to have, in different places, or as seen by observers from different places, *a* may be *F* and not-*F*, or may appear to be *F* and not-*F* on the fourth of the above grounds: at different locations, and as observed from different positions.[2]

Now if Plato were dictating this account, he would have certainly wanted us to include the third of the above grounds: the one represented in the *Hippias Major* by the girl who is supposed to be beautiful and not beautiful, because she is more beautiful than other girls but less beautiful than a goddess; in the *Phaedo* by Simmias, supposed to be tall and not tall, because he is taller than Socrates but less tall than Phaedo; in the *Theaetetus* (154c–155b), by the six dice, which are supposed to be both numerous and not numerous, because they are more numerous than four dice and less numerous than twelve. It should be evident from these examples that here Plato suffers from a certain confusion. From

(P) *x* is more *F* than *y*, and less *F* than *z*,

he infers

(Q) *x* is *F* and not-*F*.

And *Q* does *not*, of course, follow from *P*. For just suppose that Simmias were 6 feet 5 inches tall, and Phaedo 6 feet 6 inches. Simmias, then, would still be shorter than Phaedo. But would anyone want to call him "short" on that account? It is clear from just this that there is something wrong with Plato's inference; or, more precisely, something misleading about it. It would be far worse, viciously wrong, if *Q* were meant to express a self-contradiction. But I think it is clear that Plato does not mean any-

[1] Or even *F* and not-*F* in respect of the same character—e.g. one part of it hot, another cold. Cf. p. 10, n. 3. above.
[2] Cf. *Prot.* 356c; *Rep.* 602c; *Phil.* 41e–42a.

thing so extreme.[1] This we can tell from his own statement of the principle of non-contradiction at *Rep.* 436e:

> The same thing can never act or be acted upon in contrary ways, or have contrary properties [literally: 'or be opposites'], at the same time, in the same respect, and in relation to the same thing.

To run afoul of this principle Simmias would have to be tall and short in relation *to the same person*, which he obviously is not. We should, therefore, not take Q at face value, but read it only as an ellipsis for

(R) x is F in relation to y, and not-F in relation to z.

Put in this way, there is obviously no contradiction at all.[2] Then our only remaining objection is to the use of statements of the form of (Q) as ellipses for statements of the form of (R). That the language (English or Greek) will not always allow "x is F", as an ellipsis for "x is F in relation to y" should be sufficiently clear from the example I have just used. Anyone who knew that Simmias was 6 feet 5 inches, but still declared that he was short, and then explained, when challenged, that he only meant that Simmias was short by comparison with Phaedo, would be thought a liar, unless he could be let off as a practical joker. So, too, would one who, knowing that Helen is the most beautiful woman that ever lived, said with a straight face that she is ugly on no better grounds than that she is ugly by comparison with Aphrodite.

Let us then offer Plato a little advice as to how he might improve the intelligibility of his theory: 'Rest your case for the applicability of the F and not-F formula to sensible particulars,' we might tell him, 'on the three grounds you gave us a moment ago, and drop this one. For if you stick to those others, no one could misunderstand you to mean that sensible particulars are logical monstrosities, systematically violating the principle of non-contradiction. Nothing of this sort would be suggested by the fact that a particular is F in one respect, not-F in another; or F at one time, not-F at another; or F at one place, not-F at another. That you did not think of particulars as violating the principle of non-contradiction seems clear to us from the fact that when you

[1] Cf. Adam's note on *Rep.* 479a.
[2] Cf. W. D. Ross, *Plato's Theory of Ideas*, Oxford, 1951, p. 38; G. E. L. Owen, "A Proof in the Περὶ Ἰδεῶν", *Journal of Hellenic Studies* 67, (1957), Part One, pp. 103 ff., at pp. 108–9.

declare the principle inviolate at *Rep.* 436e, your own example is a
sensible particular, a spinning top. And this must have been no
less clear to your own contemporaries; none of them got the
impression that you thought sensible things self-contradictory—
a doctrine that would have startled them fully as much as it would
us, and earned you a leading place among the stultifiers of human
reason in Book Γ of the *Metaphysics*. That being the case, you had
better make it clear that you would not offer "Simmias is tall and
not tall", "Six dice are numerous and not numerous", etc., as
examples of what you mean by the *F* and not-*F* predicament in
which sensibles are involved. You do not need this form of argument, since the other three grounds suffice to make the case for
your contention that the *F* and not-*F* formula applies to sensibles,
but never to Forms. For this contention the "Simmias is tall and
not-tall" type of argument is worse than useless: it is self-
defeating. For in this respect particulars *cannot* be systematically
differentiated from Forms; some Forms could also be said to be *F*
and not-*F* on exactly the same ground.[1] For the number (i.e. the
Form), *Six*, is greater than *Four* and smaller than *Twelve*; and the
kind (i.e. the Form), *Quadruped*, is greater than *Horse*,[2] but smaller
than *Animal*. So on that reckoning the Forms, *Six*, and *Quadruped*, would each be great and not great. This type of argument
then had better be dropped. Or, if you must keep it, modify it so
as to make it apply only in the case of *causally effective* relations.
There you can find all the cases you want for *x* being *F* in one
relation, not-*F* in another—e.g. Simmias, normally dry, not dry
when immersed in water. This would bring out perfectly your
contention by showing that Simmias, unlike the Forms he in-
stantiates, is susceptible of genuinely contrary predications in
suitably different (causal) relations to other things.' I submit that
Plato would have good reason to accept this advice, and that we
have good reason for offering it to him. For its effect would be to
free his theory from an incidental blemish and make it appear to
best advantage. In this way we would insure that our criticism

[1] Cf. the difficulty pointed out by Professor Demos: Allen *op. cit.*, p. 333,
n. 13.

[2] Where *B*, not co-extensive with *A*, is logically included by *A*, Plato
speaks of *A*'s "containing" (περιέχειν) *B*, and of *B* as a "part" (μέρος, μόριον)
of *A*. *A* would then be "greater" than *B* as a whole is greater than any of its
parts. Plato accordingly speaks of "great" or "small" kinds, or parts of
kinds, in the *Politicus* (e.g. 262a, 265a).

would not be wasted on superficial errors, but on the enduringly important and interesting aspect of the theory. To this I now turn, but with the utmost brevity, for a thorough discussion of the relevant issues is quite impossible within the space at my disposal.

III

On the interpretation of Plato's theory I have offered, the grounds on which sensible particulars are judged to be less real than their respective Forms coincide very largely (and, if my proposed emendation were accepted, would coincide completely) with those categorical features which disqualify them for serving as objects of a certain kind of knowledge: knowledge which, Plato says, has "infallibility", or, in less inflated, more exact, terms for what he means, logical certainty. Nothing can qualify as a cognoscendum for this purpose if it is concrete, temporal, spatial, and caught in chains of physical causation—if it is cluttered up with contingent characters. All of its properties must stick to it with logical glue, so that they can never get unstuck with changes in time, spatial location, or causal environment. It must be eternally invariant and as logically transparent as geometrical concepts come to be when all of their properties have been exhibited as the necessary consequences of their formal inter-connections. Thus it must possess those very features which are the defining characteristics of the Platonic Form. In recognising only one kind of knowledge— knowledge of objects having these, and only these, features— Plato had no choice but to say that only the Forms were completely, or purely, or perfectly "real" in the sense I have been investigating in this paper: cognitively reliable. Thus the degrees-of-reality doctrine is, in this respect, a lucid consequence of Plato's epistemology. Recognising only one kind of knowledge, Plato had no choice but to recognise only one kind of full or complete reality.

To put the matter in this way shows, I think, a fruitful direction our criticism of Plato may take. Instead of merely protesting his down-grading of the reality of the sensible world, we can show on what conditions Plato himself would have had cause to upgrade it: i.e. if he could have seen that this sensible world, such unpromising material for logical analysis, is the best possible material for that very different cognitive venture which, when successful, results in *empirical* knowledge. If we want this sort of knowledge, its only possible subject-matter would consist of those very things we observe by the senses, or hypothesise to explain what we so observe, and whose properties we record in empirically confirm-able or disconfirmable propositions. For this purpose the Platonic Forms are grotesquely unsuitable, and would have to be judged vastly less "real" than physical objects, stuffs or processes—mere ghostly replicas of them. We would thus be offering Plato not so much a refutation of his theory, as an extension of it, though ad-mittedly one whose results he would find disconcerting. For if he were to accept this offer he would then have to rule, with equally good reason, that Forms are both "more" and "less" real than their sensible instances, since they would now turn out to be more dependable than they for one purpose, less so for another. And if we could persuade him to come so far, we might then try to talk him into a further step, suggesting to him that "more real" and "less real" are themselves rather misleading expressions in this context. Would it not be better to drop these comparatives, and say outright that only the Forms are "real" as judged by the criteria of the kind of knowledge which aspires to logical certainty, while only sensibles are "real" as judged by the very different criteria of empirically testable knowledge?

No one, I trust, will object that if Plato were to assent to such a proposal he would no longer be the Plato of the dialogues, the "real" Plato of historical research. This should be only too obvious. My reason for playing with these wild counterfactuals was not to rewrite, but to illuminate, the philosophy Plato left us. By looking at it from this perspective we have a better chance to understand one of its major achievements: its exploration— the first of its kind in Western philosophy, and a largely, if not wholly, successful one—of the categorical differences between things like Beauty, Justice, Triangularity, and the like, and those individuals, states, events, processes of which such general terms can be predicated. Plato showed that all, and only, the first had to be non-sensible, incorporeal, incomposite, timeless, spaceless, incapable of causal agency, structured eternally by logical chains of entailment and bars of incompatibility. In getting results such as these, while working with the crudest of tools against formid-able obstacles of ingrained linguistic habits, Plato must be rated one of the great explorers in the world of thought. To see that he got these results from a *degrees*-of-reality theory, while all he needed was a *kinds*-of-reality theory, will help us to recognise the ways, good and bad, in which his theory served him. Certainly a kinds-of-reality theory would have served him much better as an instrument of categorical inquiry. One has a better chance to see and state correctly the differences between particulars and universals, if one expects in advance that both will be equally "real" in their different ways. For then one will not be tempted to misconstrue universals as a higher grade of particulars, or think of sensible particulars as inferior "imitations" or "copies" of Ideal Forms. Plato did not wholly resist this temptation, and it was then that the most serious of his logical mishaps befell him.[1] To that extent the degrees of reality theory was not an unmixed asset. But to operate with mixed assets seems to be unavoidable in the highly speculative business of metaphysics.[2]

[1] Cf. R. Robinson, *Plato's Earlier Dialectic* (Revised Edition, Oxford, 1953), pp. 260–2; Vlastos, "The Third Man Argument in the Parmenides," *Philos. Review* 63 (1954), pp. 319 ff.; A. Wedberg, *Plato's Philosophy of Mathematics* (Stockholm, 1955), pp. 36–8.

[2] I am much indebted to Mr. B. A. O. Williams for useful criticism of an earlier draft which led me to make some improvements.

PLATO AND THE
MATHEMATICIANS[1]
R. M. Hare

IN *Rep.* 510b ff., in a passage which is too well known to require
quoting in full, Plato finds fault with mathematics, or at least
with the mathematicians of his day. It is the purpose of this article
to discuss briefly the question, What fault?—a question which has
excited a great deal of controversy among scholars, but which
cannot be satisfactorily answered without broaching, as I shall do,
some substantial philosophical problems.

Plato's indictment of the mathematicians rests upon two main
counts: that they use physical diagrams, and that in their studies
the mind 'is compelled to make its enquiry starting from *hypotheses*,[2] and proceeding not beginningwards but endwards'. Since
these two grounds of attack are obscure (and are admitted by
Plato to be obscure: 'I don't quite understand', says Glaucon), let
us leave for the moment the question of what the *hypotheses* were,
and the other question of what was wrong with using diagrams,
and turn to the next thing which he says. This is, that the mathematicians 'do not, after that, think it requisite to give, either to
themselves or to others, any account of these *hypotheses*, as being
evident to everybody'. It is, perhaps, not so difficult to find out

[1] I have, while acknowledging my own responsibility for the many errors
which will surely be found in this paper, to thank Mr. Richard Robinson,
Professor Anders Wedberg, and the editor for their encouragement and
helpful criticism. I have also to express my pleasure at finding so much to
agree with in Mr. Bluck's commentaries on the *Phaedo* and *Meno*, which I
read after these ideas had occurred to me.

[2] I shall print this word consistently in italics, to avoid the temptation to
assume that it means 'hypotheses' in any of its modern senses.

what Plato meant by 'give an account (*logon didonai*)' because in a later passage, in which the wording is very closely parallel, he amplifies this point (533b ff.). There he says that mathematics 'dreams about that which is, but cannot see it with eyes awake, so long as it leaves undisturbed the *hypotheses* which it uses, and cannot give an account of them'. The 'so long as' here suggests that this defect of mathematics is remediable by undertaking the more fundamental enquiry which he calls 'dialectic'.

In the passage which follows (especially 534b ff.) Plato says that the dialectician is the man who, unlike the mathematicians he has been attacking, 'demands, in the case of each thing, an account of its being (*logos tês ousiâs*)'; and he says, in language which echoes 510c, that 'the man who cannot give a *logos* to himself and to another, to that extent lacks understanding (*nous*)' of the thing in question (cf. 511d). In the immediately following and 'analogous (*hôsautôs*)' remarks about the Idea of the Good in particular, he uses the phrase 'to define by the *logos* the Idea of the Good, distinguishing it from all the other things'. Now, even if we did not know that the expression '*logos tês ousiâs*' became, for Aristotle, a technical term, which we translate 'real (or essential) definition', it would be fairly clear from these remarks that '*logon didonai*' means 'to give a definition of', in that sense of 'definition' in which to give one is to answer the question, so closely associated with Socrates, 'What is . . . ?' followed by the name of the thing under discussion. If any confirmation of this conjecture be needed, we have it in 533b, where, instead of 'demand, in the case of each thing, a *logos* of its being', Plato gives what can only be an alternative formulation of the same point: 'demand concerning what each thing is'. There he is explicitly contrasting dialectic with mathematics.

Returning now to 510c, we bring with us a clue to the identity of the *hypotheses* mentioned in that passage. For, whatever they are, they must be things of which (or about which) it is possible to give a *logos*; and this, we now see, means 'to say what they are'. Commentators have spent much time asking what *propositions* Plato can be referring to under the name 'hypotheses', and have suggested various more or less forced ways of interpreting the examples which he gives ('the odd and the even, and the figures, and the three kinds of angles, and other things like these') in order to extract from them propositions of some kind or another. But one cannot ask the question 'What is it?' of a proposition (e.g. the proposition that there are just three kinds of angles, or the proposition that the triangle is a three-sided rectilinear figure). Of a proposition, the appropriate question would be 'Is it true?' or 'Why is it true?'. The question 'What is it?' can be appropriately asked only of a *thing*. It seems to follow that Plato means just what he says in his list of examples. Of all these things (the odd and the even, etc.), it is perfectly appropriate to ask 'What are they?'; and if we found Socrates asking such a question in one of the dialogues, we should not be in the least surprised. The reasons why it has not always been realised that the *hypotheses* here must be things, not propositions, seem to be two. The first, which is not important, is the seductive associations of the modern word 'hypothesis'. The second is that there is a very long history of 'hypothesis' meaning some kind of propositional assumption, going back to Aristotle, and, indeed, to Plato himself. In some passages in Aristotle and Plato, '*hypotheses*' are certainly propositions of some kind. But, for the reason given, it is impossible for them to be propositions here, though, as we shall see, they bring certain propositional assumptions with them.

It requires explaining how Plato can here speak of *hypotheses* as things, whereas elsewhere, and indeed perhaps elsewhere in the *Republic*, he seems to speak of them as propositions. The explanation is that in Plato the whole conception of knowledge is in a process of transition which he but dimly understood. In the *Republic* and elsewhere he frequently speaks of knowledge as if it were something analogous to sight, save that it is done not with the physical eye but with 'the eye of the mind', and that the object of this 'seeing' is not a physical object but an Idea. There has been a long transition, begun perhaps in Plato but not complete even now, from this paradigm of knowledge (knowledge, by acquaintance, of an object) to another, which might be described as 'propositional knowledge'. This is the kind of knowledge that we have when we are able truly and with certainty to *say* that something is the case. Logic cannot get very far so long as the more primitive paradigm of knowledge by acquaintance is dominant; much that is obscure in Plato becomes clearer when we realise that he is trying to give an account of logical relations between propositions on the model of quasi-physical 'connections' between things (the Ideas) which are seen with the mind's eye. What he is talking about, for example, in *Rep.* 511b ff. is the ancestor of what we now call 'deduction'; but it is not, and cannot be, deduction as we know it, because it is conceived of, not as the discovery of a relation between propositions or even between facts, but as the quasi-physical seeing or even grasping of the quasi-visible or quasi-tangible connections between transcendental objects.

The same holds good of knowledge of any sort, including knowledge of the Ideas themselves. The Ideas are things, not propositions. The definitions of them are propositions, and it is the job of the dialectician to discover these; but the objects of knowledge (recorded in definitions) are entities (e.g. the Good) which can be 'caught hold of' (511b) or 'looked at' (518c and *passim*). The kind of knowledge which Plato called *noêsis* was knowledge by acquaintance of a thing, not knowledge that a certain proposition was true, though the knowledge could be expressed in a proposition or *logos* (viz. the definition of the thing). The very word which we translate 'truth' (*alêtheiâ*) means as often as not 'genuineness' (a property of a thing), and is the equivalent of '*ousiâ*' (the property of really existing)—cf. *Rep.* 524e 1 with 527b 9; and see also 525c 6.

It is not, therefore, surprising that on occasion Plato speaks of *hypotheses*, which are a kind of surrogate or second-class object of knowledge, as if they, like the objects of the best sort of knowledge, were a class of things. They are, in fact, surrogate or supposititious Ideas (at any rate in the passages we have been considering). No doubt much that is said in this—to us—primitive language could be more clearly said in the language of propositions. But we must not read too much into Plato—at least, we must not do so unguardedly, without realising that, though he was starting a great deal, he did live a very long time ago. The seeds of nearly all philosophy are to be discovered in Plato, but we must not pretend that they are more than seeds, which require the closest of scrutiny before even one who knows what they grew into can see the relation between them and it.

All this, however, does not make much clearer what, according to Plato, the mathematicians are doing, and what he thinks is wrong with it. To understand this, it may help to turn to the longest piece of mathematics that has come down to us from Plato's time, namely the well-known 'Slave' passage in the *Meno* (82a ff.). It may be that, although it is Socrates himself who is eliciting the mathematics from the Slave, the faults which Plato mentions in the *Republic* are there exhibited. There is some indication, in the fact that the example (square and diagonal) used in the *Meno* is the same as that in *Rep.* 510d, that Plato may have had the *Meno* passage in mind when he wrote the *Republic* passage; but it would be unwise to put any weight on this.

Socrates asks first whether the Slave speaks Greek. This is a matter of some significance (which may or may not have escaped Plato); for a rigorous geometrical demonstration depends on logic, and logic depends (in some sense, which I shall not try to make precise) on language. The geometry which is subsequently done is, as we shall see, not entirely rigorous, and depends partly upon the empirical observation of drawn figures; but even for this the Slave has to know a language—he has to be able to *recognise* the figure drawn on the sand as that to which the name 'square' can be applied.

What then happens is that Socrates draws a square and asks, 'Tell me, boy, do you know a square, that it is like this (*toiouton*)?' The Slave says that he does. Socrates then says, 'A square figure, *therefore*, is one which has all these lines equal, being four in number?' (my italics). The Slave agrees. But already we have had something which ought to make any geometer wince who has some regard for rigour. What is the 'therefore' doing? How does the Slave know that the sides of a square are equal? How, even, does he know that a square is 'like this'? How, that is to say, does he know that the figure which Socrates has drawn *is* a square? And what follows is as bad. Socrates goes on, 'Isn't it one, too, which has these lines across the middle equal?' After the Slave has swallowed this, he says, 'There could be, *therefore*, a figure like this that was larger, and one that was smaller?'

We do not need to read further; the general point has already become clear that a great deal is being *taken for granted*. A rigorous geometer who wanted to prove theorems about the square would have to include in his premises the *definition* of 'square'. In modern terms, it is because we mean by 'square', 'rhombus with equal diagonals' (or, alternatively, 'rectangle with equal sides'), and mean by these other terms what is laid down in their definitions,

C   25

that we can prove the various theorems about the square. If the 'lines across the middle' are taken to be diagonals, then Socrates has at least included in his remarks the two constituents of a possible definition of 'square' ('rhombus with equal diagonals'). But even so, that a square must have these properties is being taken for granted, not shown to hold. If, as appears to be the more popular view, these lines are transversals joining the mid-points of the sides of the square, the proceeding lacks even this element of rigour.

To take another example, it is because we mean by 'circle', 'locus of a point, in a plane, equidistant from a given point' (cf. *Ep*. VII, 342b), that we can prove the various theorems about the circle. Any of the proofs will contain a premiss to the effect that two lines are equal because they are radii of the circle; and this we know because we know, as Plato would have put it, what the Circle *is*. Socrates perhaps knew what the Square is; but there is nothing to show that the Slave did. All he does is to recognise a drawn figure as a square (most improperly, from the Platonic point of view, since no drawn figure is perfectly square), and then to agree to the general statement that squares have certain properties. This may be one reason why Socrates himself says in 85c, at the end of the lesson, that the Slave has as yet only true belief, not knowledge; the language is like that of *Rep*. 533b, already quoted. 'So then,' says Socrates, 'he is in a state of not knowing, and yet there are in him true beliefs about these things which he does not know? . . . And now these beliefs have been made to rise up in him like a dream. But if someone asks him these same things many times and in many ways, in the end, you may be sure, he will have as exact knowledge about them as anybody.' Here there is a hint (not the only one in the *Meno*) of what is to come in the *Republic*: to turn true belief into knowledge, dream into waking vision, the sedulous practice of dialectic is required.

But as it stands the geometry lesson in the *Meno* is open to all the strictures that Plato brings against mathematicians in the *Republic*, and helps us to understand those strictures by illustrating the faults against which they are brought. Socrates and the Slave take a figure (an example of 'the figures' mentioned as *hypotheses* in *Rep*. 510c), 'act as if they had knowledge of it, make it their *hypothesis*' (i.e. take for granted that they have got something to talk about), 'do not after that think it requisite to give . . . any *logos* of it, as being evident to everybody' (there it is, they might say, on the sand), 'but, starting from it, they now go through all the rest of their stuff and end in mutual agreement at whatever it was they set out to enquire into'. The word which I have rendered 'in mutual agreement' (*homologoumenôs*) might mean 'in agreement or consistency with their premisses'; and the same is true of the similar phrase in 533c; but since, as we have seen, an important feature of the 'Slave' passage is that for want of rigour Socrates and the Slave make do with mutual agreement, it is tempting to take it in the former way, although it spoils an equally tempting parallel with Frege (see p. 28).

Why is it that the Slave does not see that more is required than the bare assertion that squares have certain properties? The answer—as I have already hinted—is connected with the other criticism which Plato brings against the mathematicians in 510d. Because he is using a visible figure which does appear to have the characteristics which are said to belong to squares, it is easy for him to assume that no further investigation is required. Socrates' initial gambit shows this: he seems to argue 'You recognise this (the drawn figure) as a square; *therefore* a square figure is one which has all these four lines equal.' There could hardly be a better illustration of the mistake that Plato is exposing in the *Republic*; a general proposition, which should be known *a priori* and by definition, is asserted merely on the basis of the empirical inspection of a single, particular, hastily drawn figure. When he wrote the *Republic*, Plato had come to think (rightly) that geometers must do better than this; and he may have been dimly aware of it even when he wrote the *Meno*.

To sum up our conclusions so far, we may say that what is wrong with the mathematicians, in Plato's view, is that they employ concepts like 'square', and assert propositions containing them, without, as a rigorous thinker must, proving these propositions on the basis of the definitions of the concepts—and that they are led to act in this way because they are using physical diagrams and taking as true what seems to be true of the diagrams. In order to sustain my thesis, it is not necessary for me to claim that definitions were never given by the mathematicians of Plato's time. There is some evidence that they sometimes were. All that is necessary for the truth of the thesis is that the essential logical rôle of definitions in proof should not have been realised, and that therefore mathematicians were casual about supplying and justifying them, and often omitted to do so altogether. To suppose that this was so is at least plausible, if we consider that Frege is able to make much the same complaint even about the mathematicians of a more recent time, in the well-known introduction to *Foundations of Arithmetic*. Frege was, in many ways, of a highly Platonic cast of mind, and these pages are sprinkled with passages which have (whether intentionally or unintentionally) a Platonic or Socratic ring—for example, 'The first prerequisite for learning anything is thus utterly lacking—I mean, the knowledge that we do not know.'[1] Frege begins by criticising mathematicians for employing the symbol '1' without asking what it means, or what the number one is. He protests (as Plato would have) against the identification of the number one with any of the things that are said to be 'one thing'. '"$1^1 = 1$" asserts nothing of the Moon, nothing of the Sun, nothing of the Sahara, nothing of the Peak of Teneriffe; for what could be the sense of any such assertion?'

'Questions like these,' he goes on [i.e. like, 'What is the number one?'], 'catch even mathematicians for that matter, or most of them, unprepared with any satisfactory answer. Yet is it not a scandal that our science should be so unclear about the first and foremost among its objects, and one which is apparently so simple? Small hope, then, that we shall be able to say what number is.' His own programme for putting arithmetic on a sound footing involved, above all, the defining of the key concepts in it —and rightly so, because unless we have these definitions (either explicit, or implicit by means of axioms) the science will altogether lack rigour. 'The rigour of the proof remains an illusion, however flawless the chain of deductions, so long as the definitions are justified only as an after-thought by our failing to come across any contradiction' (and still more so, he might have added, if they are not put in at all). 'By these methods we shall, at bottom, never have achieved more than an empirical certainty, and we must really face the possibility that we may still in the end encounter a contradiction which brings the whole edifice down in ruins.'[2]

[1] *Op. cit.*, tr. Austin, p. iii; cf. *Meno* 84a–c.
[2] *Op. cit.*, p. ix; cf. p. 27 above.

On Plato's theory there is even greater need for definitions than there is on Frege's theory, because definitions had in Plato's thought an ontological as well as a logical rôle to play. The kind of definition which Socrates invented, and which established itself in the systems of Plato and Aristotle, was what we call the essential or real definition—the statement, as Aristotle put it, of 'what it was, for a certain thing, to be' (or possibly 'to be what it was': e.g. of 'what it was, for a coat, to be a coat'). It was therefore natural for Plato to think that, by defining some Idea, one had proved that it existed—that by saying *what* it was, one had proved *that* it was. Aristotle saw that there was a distinction between these two things (*An. Post.* 72a 23); but Plato may have been misled by the analogy which he sometimes draws between knowing Ideas and knowing, e.g. people (cf. *Meno* 71b). This analogy is of a piece with his tendency to treat Ideas as transcendent supremely perfect *individuals*. If one knows that a person is of a certain sort, one must (he might have argued) know, *a fortiori*, that he exists; and there is in this case justification for arguing thus, because, as Mr. Strawson has recently reminded us, if we say that the King of France is wise we imply, in some sense, that he exists.[1] It is illegitimate to extend this form of argument to things like 'the Circle' (at least if we think we are establishing the existence of anything more than an *ens rationis*); if we can say what the circle is, this only establishes the possibility of speaking in a certain way, and does nothing to establish the existence of a transcendent entity called 'The Circle'. But it would have been consistent with Plato's whole outlook to think that it did establish this.

A further source of confusion may have been the following. Plato, when he wrote the *Republic*, was not clear about the distinction between the existential 'is' and the 'is' of predication. Thus, in 479b, c, he seems not to distinguish between saying that a eunuch is not a man and saying that he (*simpliciter*, as Aristotle would have put it) is not. By the time he wrote the latter part of the *Sophist* (which may be, among other things, an attempt to grapple with this problem), Plato had perhaps become a little clearer that there was a distinction—but not so clear as Aristotle

---

[1] 'On Referring', *Mind*, 1950 (also in *Essays in Conceptual Analysis*, ed. A. G. N. Flew, Macmillan, 1956). The differences between Strawson and Russell are irrelevant to the present point.

shows himself to be in *Sophistical Refutations* 167a 2. Plato may have thought, therefore, that, if I know that the circle is the locus of a point, etc., I thereby know that the circle is, *simpliciter* (i.e. that it exists). If this conjecture is right, it would explain Plato's insistence on the three-way connection between a thing's existing, its being knowable, and the ability of the knower to give a *logos* of it (cf. *Rep.* 534b, c, *Meno* 98a, *Rep.* 477a).

It remains to ask whether Plato thought that these defects in mathematics were remediable, and if so how. There is evident a certain tension in his attitude to the subject. On the one hand he describes its practitioners as 'dreaming about that which is'; on the other, he made it, in his programme of education, an absolutely obligatory 'hauling-tackle' to drag people towards reality (524e, cf. 523a). There are two plausible explanations. The first is that in 510b ff. Plato is attacking the mathematicians of his day, and implying that, if they were to reform their ways, mathematics could take its place as a branch of knowledge. 'Reform their ways' would mean, 'subject mathematics to the logical discipline of dialectic, insisting on having definitions of the key concepts, and on relating these definitions to that of the master-key, the Good; and thus dispensing with the visual aids on which they now rely'. The second explanation is that Plato thought that mathematics was inherently and irremediably defective in certain respects (viz. that it could not avoid using drawn figures, and had to get on without the support of a knowledge of the relevant Ideas), but nevertheless was valuable as a propaedeutic to the study of dialectic.

In 510b and 511a it is said that in mathematics the mind is 'compelled' to proceed in the way it does; and not much of a hint is given of how the practice of dialectic would improve the procedures of mathematics itself. On the other hand, it may be argued that 'compelled' means no more than 'compelled by the faulty procedures currently adopted'. In 511c, Plato says that mathematicians, 'because they look at [the objects of their study] not by going up to a beginning, but starting from *hypotheses*, seem to you not to have understanding (*nous*) about them, although they are intelligible (*noêta*) if linked with a beginning'. The meaning of the last phrase is disputed; but one possible interpretation of it is that, once mathematics is 'connected up' by dialectic with the Idea of the Good, it becomes a branch of knowledge proper. This is supported by 533c: 'it cannot see with eyes awake, *so long as* it leaves undisturbed the *hypotheses* which it uses'. This seems to imply that once the *hypotheses* are 'disturbed', dream may yield to reality. And in the *Meno* passage, as we saw, it is said that the true opinion which the Slave has is capable of being turned into knowledge by a longer course of questioning (85c).

We may perhaps take it, then, that the first of the defects of mathematics, that which consists in its wrong use of *hypotheses*, is ultimately remediable, though no doubt inescapable in the initial stages of instruction. What of the second defect—the use of figures? If to give up the use of figures in geometry would be to do analytical geometry, expressed by means of algebraical symbols alone, then it would be anachronistic to suppose that Plato had any such thing in mind—although the line of thought which he was starting, with its insistence on logical as opposed to empirical proofs, led ultimately to this conclusion. But we must not be confused here by an assumption which commentators have been too ready to make, namely, that among the figures that Plato wished to reject are to be included, not only figures drawn on the sand, but also figures looked at with the mind's eye—i.e. what we should call, though Plato would not have, 'imagined figures'. There is no indication in the text that Plato frowned on the use of the latter. Indeed, there is some evidence that he thought of looking at things with the mind's eye as a paradigm of true knowledge,[1] and as what ought to take the place of looking at physical things (e.g. drawn figures) with the physical eye, when empirical observation gave way to logical thought. If this view is correct, then Plato may have considered that the empirical procedures of current mathematics could be superseded, without having thought of anything so advanced as analytical geometry.

We may, then, hazard a guess that Plato thought both the defects of contemporary mathematics remediable ultimately by the help of dialectic, though unavoidable in the schoolroom. But how did he think that dialectic could help? To ask this is to raise a very large question, about which, since it is still very obscure to me, I can only make some tentative suggestions. The remarks which I have made about the mathematicians' *hypotheses* and their use of

[1] See my article in *The Critical Approach: Essays in honour of Karl Popper*, ed. M. Bunge.

them are not intended to apply to the dialecticians' use of the same (or it may be different) *hypotheses*. It may be that these latter, unlike the *hypotheses* mentioned in 510c, *are* some kind of *logoi* or propositions—though there are difficulties in this view, and I have found no strong support for it in the text of this passage. In the *Phaedo*, likewise, it may be that the *hypotheses* referred to are *logoi* (though Mr. Bluck seems to argue against this view; see his *Phaedo*, p. 165). In the *Meno*, where *hypotheses* are said to be used by mathematicians and where one is used by Socrates in his argument, they seem to be propositions, as even Mr. Bluck evidently agrees— but, lest this should be taken as casting doubt on what I have said about the mathematicians' use of *hypotheses* in the *Republic*, it must be pointed out that it is hard to find much similarity between what the mathematicians are said to be doing with their *hypotheses* in the *Meno*, and what they are said to be doing with them in the *Republic*, or even between the *hypotheses* themselves (*Meno*, 86e ff.).

What is the dialectician supposed to be achieving, and how is this going to help the mathematician? We have already seen that it is the aim of the dialectician to establish definitions. If this is so, his task is a good deal easier than it would be on some other views about what he is trying to do. It is not possible to explain why, without a short excursus into the relations between logic and metaphysics. Metaphysics, or much of it, is logic in ontological dress; it is logic done in the material mode of speech. For example, when Socrates asks 'What is mud (or clay)?' and gives the answer 'Earth mixed with water' (*Theaet.* 147a), the status of both the question and the answer is equivocal. There is no doubt that Plato and Aristotle would have regarded the definitions which are the answers to such questions as synthetic statements about the natures or essences of the *definienda*, which for Plato were Ideas. Yet they are also thought of as having the *a priori* character which belongs to definitions in most modern senses of the word. That is to say, once we realise that mud *is* earth mixed with water, we are supposed to know this as a necessary truth about mud. In short, the Socratic-Platonic-Aristotelian essential definition, the archetype of all synthetic *a priori* propositions, tries to have it both ways. It tries both to be a synthetic statement about an existing thing (in Plato's case, an Idea), and to have the necessity of a definition (or, to be more accurate, of something that is true by definition). It would be out of place to argue here the question whether there can be any such synthetic *a priori* truths; for our historical purpose it is enough to assume that Plato thought that there could, and to ask how it made the dialectician's task seem easier to him than it might to a modern.

Those who believe in the possibility of synthetic *a priori* truths are accustomed, when it comes to discovering or proving them, to lean heavily on their *a priori* character. That is to say, they use arguments which, although they are supposed to prove something synthetic, in fact consist covertly or overtly in appeals to language and meaning. Thus, if anybody denied that mud was earth mixed with water, it might be said that if anything were earth mixed with water it must be mud, and vice versa—and this would be said with the implication that anybody who doubted it just couldn't be understanding the words.[1] Now if it were avowed that what was being asserted was that 'mud' *meant* 'earth mixed with water' (if, that is to say, the synthetic character of the conclusion to be established were given up), this would be a perfectly legitimate argument. I want to maintain that Plato's suggested procedure is covertly linguistic in character, though he himself did not understand this.

Let us take as an example the definition of the Circle. Suppose that a dialectician has this word '*kyklos*' (meaning as much 'wheel' as 'circle'), which is in common use, and asks himself the question 'What, really, *is* the *kyklos*?' Now no doubt Plato thought that the dialectician would be asking this question about a real object of thought transcending this world, and that the answer would be a synthetic statement; but, nevertheless, in arriving at and testing such a definition by dialectical methods he would be, unwittingly perhaps, appealing to the ordinary use of the word, or a tidied-up version of it. He would propound suggested definitions, and see whether, when the word was used in the way suggested, it led to absurdities—i.e. to things that, since words mean what they do, nobody would be willing to say. If this were what the dialectician was doing, he would be following a method in philosophy which

[1] We may ignore, as irrelevant to our present problem, another possible interpretation of the statement 'Mud is earth mixed with water': viz. as meaning 'If one takes a certain recognisable substance called earth and mixes it with another called water, the result will always be some stuff of the sort called mud; and this is the only way of producing this stuff.' So interpreted, it is an empirical proposition. It is confusion with this quite different proposition that enables the definition to masquerade as synthetic.

seems a good one and still has many adherents.[1] And this view is
supported by the fact that the definitions which Plato gives us
(e.g. 'Mud is earth mixed with water' and 'The circle is the locus
of a point equidistant, etc.'—to say nothing of those in the
Academic dictionary called *Definitions*, many of which no doubt
go back to him) are such as would very naturally and properly be
established by such a method. It seems to be this kind of procedure that is being referred to in *Rep.* 534b ff., and we see it
actually in operation in *Rep.* 331c and elsewhere.

It has often been objected to such a method (substantially
similar to the Socratic elenchus) that, relying as it does on the
mere failure to refute a proposed view, it does nothing to establish its truth; for it is one thing to fail to show that a view is false,
and another to show positively that it is true. When what we are
trying to establish are definitions, however, it is not clear that this
objection is well taken. It is not even clear that it is a fair one in
some other fields; scientists, according to Professor Popper,[2]
never prove their hypotheses but only fail, after trying hard, to
falsify them. This analogy with scientific method may show (however reluctant Plato would have been to admit it) that there is after
all an empirical element in the elenchus; are we not, in practising
it, looking for possible falsifications of the empirical hypothesis
that, in their ordinary discourse, people use a word in a certain
way? This problem is still a very obscure one; and it may be that
Plato could answer this last objection (see my article just referred
to).

If a group of people, who know the language in which the word
'circle' occurs, are trying to find out 'its meaning', they may think
that they have done so with sufficient certainty when they have
discovered a definition which accords with their own use of the
word, and which, try as they may, co-operatively and dialectically
—i.e. by trying out the definition in actual discourse—they cannot
fault by showing that it leads to absurdity, or to saying things
which, as they do use the word, one cannot say. It would perhaps
not be unreasonable for such a group of people, if they were un-
tutored enough to use the material mode of speech, to say that
they had discovered for certain what a circle *was*. Even now, when
linguistic philosophers have been arguing for a long time about

[1] I have discussed it, and some of the difficulties in it, in *Mind*, 1960.
[2] *The Logic of Scientific Discovery*, Hutchinson, 1956, especially pp. 32 ff.

some point of usage (for example the question 'Can I say "I intend to do A, although I am certain that I shall not succeed in doing it"?') they seem, sometimes, to satisfy themselves, justifiably or not, that they know what the right answer is. Perhaps, therefore, it was pardonable, even if in the end incorrect, for Plato to think that one could, by the method he alludes to, achieve certainty that evening *is* the ending of the day, or that wind *is* the movement of air around the earth (*Def.* 411b, c). And he may have thought that the same method was applicable to more difficult terms (including those of mathematics); here the going would be harder, but there are some gallant attempts in the *Definitions* and scattered throughout the canonical works of Plato. After all, he never claims that dialectic is easy.

One further factor (already noticed) may have made the goal of dialectic seem to Plato possible of attainment. He thought that knowledge was, like sight, some kind of apprehension of an object, but with the mind's eye. If, therefore, the dialectician was not merely submitting his *logoi* to the elenchus, but all the time searching with his mind's eye for the thing he was trying to define —as were all the participants in the discussion—and scrutinising carefully all the possible candidates, it was perhaps doubly easy for him to think that in the end they would all fix their mental eyes on the same thing, be satisfied of its genuineness, and be able to produce an indestructible definition of it. It was natural for him to conclude that, in that case, they would have achieved knowledge —especially since, in his view, they had already, in a previous existence, had knowledge of the thing and had only to recollect it.

However, we have not yet exhausted the answers to objections that Plato might have thought available to him. For he evidently thought that the pieces of knowledge, so acquired, were related to each other in some sort of system, and could therefore reinforce one another; and in particular he thought that all the other objects of knowledge (Ideas) were in some way 'attached' to the Idea of the Good (511b). We have now to ask how this helped, and in particular what was the relevance of the Idea of the Good to mathematics.

The following reflections may help us to understand Plato's thought. If we try to draw a circle, somebody may say 'That isn't a very good circle.' By this he might be taken to mean that it is not very exactly circular—that it is not the sort of circle that one would point to if one wished to give somebody an idea of what a circle was. Here 'good' seems to be being used in such a way that the criteria for being a good circle are identical with those for being (really) a circle. This use of the word (meaning roughly, 'good specimen of') is, it is hardly necessary to point out, to be distinguished from other uses more relevant to moral philosophy. There is a long line of philosophers, stretching from Plato through Aristotle and Aquinas to Mr. Geach, who have, through confusion on this point, thought that we could find out what it was to be a good man by finding out what it was to be a man.[1] Plato did not in general distinguish this use of 'good' from others; indeed, he perhaps thought that this use could, by analogy, illuminate the others. And since there was, for him, a single Idea of the Good, it was natural for him to suppose that knowledge of this Idea would put him in a position to tell good circles from bad circles, good men from bad men . . . and, in short, a good anything from a bad anything. And to know what it was to be a good φ would be to know what it was to be, really, a φ. This is implicit in his view that the Idea of anything was (perhaps among other things) the paradigm or perfectly good specimen of that kind of thing.[2]

So Plato may have argued as follows. If we wish to know what it is to be a circle (to know the Idea of circularity, or to know what the Circle is), we have to find out what it is to be a good or perfect circle. And this involves knowing the Idea of the Good, or what the Good is. Thus knowledge of the Idea of the Good is necessary to complete our knowledge of all the other Ideas. Since to be (really) a circle, a figure has to be a good circle, the Good can be said to be the source of the being and the reality of the circle—and of everything else likewise (cf. 509b and, perhaps, *Phaedo* 97e ff.). This would sufficiently explain why Plato thought the study of the Good to be the coping-stone of the mathematical sciences (534e).

Unfortunately for Plato, this line of thought is fallacious. As Aristotle saw (*Eth. Nic.* I, 6), there is no *single* quality of goodness which is possessed by all good things, and to know which would be to know what made them all good, and thus (if the confusion just mentioned be swallowed) to know what made them the

[1] See Geach's article and my reply in *Analysis*, 1956/7.
[2] See G. Vlastos, *Philosophical Review* LXIII, 1954.

things that they are. What makes a circle a good circle is *different* from what makes a square a good square or a man a good man. Aristotle's view seems to have been that the word 'good' *meant* something different in these different contexts; and in this he may have been wrong. But he was right in thinking that the *criteria* of goodness were different for different kinds of things; and this is fatal to Plato's programme. For if there is no common quality of goodness common to all good things, to know what makes two different kinds of thing good is to have two different pieces of knowledge.[1]

It might be thought that a closer understanding of the difference between the meaning of the word 'good' and the criteria for its application to different things might vitiate Aristotle's attack, and so save Plato. But this is not so. It is true that Aristotle has not demonstrated that 'good' does not have a common *meaning*, but only that there are not common criteria for its application. And so we may allow Plato the premiss that 'good' always means the same, of whatever class of objects it is used (subject to the qualification made above, that sometimes the words 'specimen of' need to be supplied). But this premiss is gained only by divorcing meaning from criteria; and so, although it may be the case that by knowing one thing—namely, what 'good' means—we shall know what it means whatever word it precedes, this will not now do for us what Plato thought it would. For to know what 'good' in 'good circle' means will not now help us to know what makes a circle a good circle. For that, we shall have to find out two more things, viz. what a circle is, and what are the qualities which make a circle a good one. And though in this particular case (because 'specimen of' is understood), these two questions may come to the same thing, there will be the further difficulty that in other cases (e.g. that of 'man') they are quite different questions.

Nevertheless, it is easy to suppose that, when he wrote the *Republic*, these difficulties had not occurred to Plato. For one of the impressions which it is hard to avoid when reading these pages is that he had not, when he wrote them, carried out in detail the programme of enquiry which he is proposing. When he did, he encountered difficulties; and that is why the account of dialectic given in later dialogues is different in many respects. Aristotle

[1] Cf. Aristotle, *Eth. Nic.* 1096a 29 ff., and my *Language of Morals*, Oxford, 1952, pp. 95 ff.

also, in trying to carry on with the Platonic programme, met with further obstacles, and his methodology becomes different again, though still related in obvious ways to Plato's. In the *Republic* we have little more than a tantalising prospectus.

If this is a defect, this article must share it; for I have not had time to undertake the detailed study which would be necessary to turn the suggestions which I have made into more than suggestions. Much remains to be discovered; and my only excuses for putting these ideas into print are, first, that I could not resist a tempting invitation to contribute to this volume, and secondly, that the work which I hope to do on this subject will be greatly assisted by such criticisms as this article may receive.

DIALECTIC
IN THE ACADEMY
Gilbert Ryle

I. ARISTOTLE'S 'ART OF DIALECTIC'

A treatise called *The Art of So and So* was a body of general rules, explanations, examples, warnings and recommendations, the study of which was calculated to help the student to become proficient in the practice in question. It was a training manual. Protagoras is said to have written an *Art of Wrestling*. Some people may learn to wrestle well from mere flair, habituation and imitation; but there is much to be learned also from the technical theory of wrestling. The same thing is true of medicine and navigation. Rule of thumb is not enough.

Between the time of Protagoras and that of Aristotle in his early teaching years, there had appeared a considerable number of *Arts of Rhetoric*. This is quite understandable since intelligent and ambitious young Greeks who looked forward to careers in public life needed to be taught how to compose forensic and political orations. Nor, save for a few specialists like mathematicians, astronomers and doctors, was any other higher education provided, until the Academy began. Not all, but many of the sophists, of whom anything is known, were, or were *inter alia*, teachers of rhetoric. The training manuals of rhetoric that Plato mentions in his *Phaedrus* (especially 266–7) were all composed by sophists. Some of these *Arts* were versified to aid memorisation by students. Aristotle, too, wrote an *Art of Rhetoric*, which we possess. But what concerns us is something different. He also wrote an *Art of Dialectic*, known to us as his *Topics*. What was the practice of dialectic of which Aristotle's *Topics* is the Art? We know what the practitioners of rhetoric practised, in what circumstances and for what professions or careers. We are not so sure what a student of the art of dialectic hoped to become a practitioner of. We know the kind of career that a Demosthenes had. Was there a corresponding kind of career for a dialectician? If not, then for whom was Aristotle providing a training manual, and for what vocation?

I mention Aristotle's *Art of Rhetoric* alongside his *Art of Dialectic* partly because Aristotle himself closely associates the two practices. (*De Arte Rhet.* Bk. I (1) 11, 12, 14; (2) 7, 8, 9, etc.; *Topics* 164a 5, 167b 8, 174b 19, 183b.) Moreover, as we shall see, the exercise which Aristotle calls 'dialectic' had been taught for a long time before Aristotle, anyhow sometimes as an ancillary to rhetoric.

What, then, is this exercise of dialectic, for which the *Topics* is a training manual? There is a special pattern of disputation, governed by strict rules, which takes the following shape. Two persons 'agree to have a battle'. One is to be questioner, the other answerer. The questioner can only ask questions; and the answerer can, with certain qualifications, answer only 'yes' or 'no'. So the questioner's questions have to be properly constructed for 'yes' or 'no' answers. This automatically rules out a lot of types of questions, like factual questions, arithmetical questions, and technical questions. Roughly it leaves us only conceptual questions, whatever these may be. The answerer begins by undertaking to uphold a certain 'thesis', e.g. that *justice is the interest of the stronger*, or that *knowledge is sense-perception*. The questioner has to try to extract from the answerer, by a series of questions, an answer or conjunction of answers inconsistent with the original thesis, i.e. drive him into an 'elenchus'. The questioner has won the duel if he succeeds in getting the answerer to contradict his original thesis, or else in forcing him to resign, or in reducing him to silence, to an infinite regress, to mere abusiveness, to pointless yammering, or to outrageous paradox. The answerer has won if he succeeds in keeping his wicket up until the close of play. The answerer is allowed to object to a question on the score that, for example, it is two or more questions in one, like *have you left off beating your father?*, or that it is metaphorical or ambiguous. The duel is fought out before an audience (cf. *Sophist* 230C); and apparently it is sometimes left to the audience to judge whether the questioner or the answerer has won. Certain debating tricks and manoeuvres are recognised as fouls. (*Topics* 171b 20; 172b 20; cf. Plato *Theaetetus* 167E). The exercise has to have a time-limit, or else the answerer can never win. I think the 'time's up' is referred to in *Topics* 161a 10 and 183a 25.

In the Greek world in general, elenctic duelling is normally called 'eristic', but this word has acquired pejorative connotations for Plato and Aristotle. They use this word and its variants for commercialised and debased forms of the exercise practised by certain sophists, who stoop to all sorts of tricks in order to make sure of winning. Plato's *Euthydemus* depicts such sophists in action. Aristotle uses the word 'dialectic' for the exercise as practised with intellectual seriousness and without conscious trickery. I shall show that Plato does so too. The word 'eristic' continues to be used, often with no pejorative connotations, after Plato's and Aristotle's time, and I shall regularly use it myself. The word 'dialectic' now carries too many daunting and uplifting associations for us to rely on it.

Why do people engage in eristic Moots? Aristotle gives several reasons:

(*a*) There is the pedagogic or tutorial motive. A student's wits are sharpened if he is made to practise argumentation by trying to defend his own theses against criticisms and by trying to think up and organise criticisms of other people's theses. So the teacher may either himself engage his pupil in eristic bouts, or else pit one pupil against another, subject to his own tutorial criticisms of their arguments. This is dialectic conducted with a *gymnastic* purpose. Obviously students may, for fun and for extra practice, conduct their own matches without tutorial supervision.

(*b*) Sometimes people are intellectually complacent or reckless. They need for the good of their souls and wits to be deflated. When they discover that they can quickly be driven, without trickery, into acknowledging things patently inconsistent with other things which they had felt perfectly sure of, they become warier and intellectually humbler. This is what Aristotle calls the *peirastic* or probing purpose. It is a part or species of the pedagogic or tutorial dialectic.

(*c*) The exercise is an absorbing game—difficult, exciting, and competitive. It has much in common with chess and fencing. It is fun to win, and fun even to try to counter one's opponent's stratagems. Aristotle calls this the *agonistic*, i.e. the match-winning purpose of the exercise. Aristotle says, what we could have guessed anyhow, that even those who dispute for intellectual gymnastic cannot be stopped from trying to win (*Topics* 164b 8–14). The students are, after all, young men; and their instructor, Aristotle, is not very old.

From Plato's *Republic* VII (537–9) (and cf. *Apology* 23C) it appears that by the composition date of this book the eristic game had acquired an unhealthy vogue; and that this had led to scandal or crisis. (See also Isocrates, *Helen* 1.) Socrates refuses to let young men engage in the exercise, though their sober seniors may do so. Apparently this really was the initial policy of the Academy. At the end of his *De Sophisticis Elenchis* Aristotle claims to have had to work out the entire *Technê* of dialectic by himself. He draws on Plato's dialogues for specimens, but he acknowledges no debts to Platonic tuition in the theory of dialectic. He received no such tuition. Plato did not teach Aristotle philosophy. This ban on eristic for young students has, however, been lifted by the time of the *Parmenides* (Part II). Now Aristotle is already teaching much of the contents of the *Topics*, and teaching it to young men.

(*d*) Some of the sophists, on occasions, put on public tournaments in which, debatably, they take on challengers from the audience, or else challenge one another. Their object is to win at all costs, and so build up such a reputation for invincibility that they will make money—make money, presumably, from the fees of the pupils who will flock for coaching in such duelling, and, conjecturally, from the gate-money paid by the audiences who come to hear the champion performing. This is the Prize-fighting or *eristic* purpose, in the pejorative sense that the word has for Plato and Aristotle.

(*e*) Finally, serious philosophers engage in duels with each other from an interest in philosophical issues themselves. Though Euthydemus and Dionysodorus may use as a mere booby-trap the question *Does not he who says that something is the case say something that is the case?*, i.e. *are not all significant statements true?*, a Plato or an Aristotle will examine this very same question in order to bring out into the light of day the relations between *significance* and *truth*. We may call this the *philosophical* purpose of the dialectical exercise. I shall have more to say later on about this function of dialectic.

In whichever of these five spirits the exercise is conducted, its rules are the same. Certain dodges, employed in sophistic duels, are disallowed in an Academic *milieu* (*Topics* 164b 8, 171b 21). We cannot from internal evidence fix the date when Aristotle composed the *Topics*. But in 354/3 B.C., i.e. some seven years before Plato's death, Isocrates, in his *Antidosis* (258–69; and cf. his *Panathenaicus* 26–9) makes it clear that the teaching of eristic is, with geometry and astronomy, already a part of the curriculum of the Academy. In the *Panathenaicus* and in his *Letter to Alexander* of 342 he is likely to be sneering at Aristotle in person as a teacher of eristic. Plato, in what must be a late, and I think is his latest finished, composition, the *Parmenides* (Part II), represents the venerated old Parmenides as demonstrating to the young Socrates the intellectual gymnastic which he must practise if he is to become a philosopher. He then produces the most unrelieved and formalised model of a two-way eristic question–answer exercise that has come down to us. The model conforms well with the rules and prescriptions collected in Aristotle's *Topics* for a philosophically serious exercise in dialectic. Plato himself does not here use the words 'dialectic', 'dialectician', or 'dialectical', or, of course, 'eristic', or 'eristical' either. There can be no reasonable doubt, then, that what Isocrates calls 'eristic' and Aristotle calls 'dialectic' is, despite the veto in *Republic* VII, being taught to young men in the Academy in or before the middle 350s; that Plato approves of this teaching; and that Aristotle teaches it, in fairly close connection with his teaching of rhetoric. It is not by coincidence that Plato unearths a coeval of Socrates called 'Aristotle' to be Parmenides' answerer. Xenocrates too must have been closely associated with the teaching of this *gymnastic*. Of his numerous writings the titles of which are recorded by Diogenes Laertius at least five have to do with dialectic, including one, in twenty books, *Of Theses*, another, in fourteen books, τῆς περὶ τὸ διαλέγεσθαι πραγματείας. At least two of the writings of Heracleides Ponticus must also be of this *genre*. That the exercise continues to be an important ingredient of university education throughout the succeeding centuries is shown by, among other things, the book-titles of the later Academics, Peripatetics and Stoics.

43

II. THE EARLIER HISTORY OF DIALECTIC

The eristic Moot was far from being the invention of Aristotle in particular or of the Academy in general. Its history goes well back into the fifth century. I set down here what I have been able to collect of its history. I shall often use the title 'eristic' for the exercise, though without the pejorative connotations which it acquired for Plato and Aristotle. It was these connotations, I guess, that made Plato coin, as Favorinus says he coined (D. L. *Plato*, 24), the noun 'dialectic', and therewith 'dialectician' and 'dialectical', from 'διαλέγεσθαι'; this last was the general verb for 'discuss', 'debate', and, specifically, 'discuss by the method of question and answer'. There are two other recurrent titles for eristic disputation. It is sometimes called '*antilogikē*', and its practitioners are described as 'antilogical' when emphasis is being laid on their readiness to argue impartially for and against any given thesis. It is sometimes called '*agonistikē*', to emphasise the fact that its practitioners are primarily out to win their matches. This match-winning spirit is regularly called 'φιλονικία' by both Plato and Aristotle. We could call it 'eristic gamesmanship'.

Diogenes Laertius credits a number of people with the invention of the eristic duel.

(a) *Zeno*. Diogenes Laertius quotes Aristotle as saying that Zeno was the inventor of dialectic; and Sextus Empiricus tells us that Aristotle said this in his *Sophist*. (See Aristotle: *Selected Fragments*.) Plato virtually says the same thing in the *Parmenides* where he makes old Parmenides tell the juvenile Socrates that if he is to become a philosopher he must put himself through a certain sort of training, namely in the method of reasoning of which Zeno has just produced an example. This method, however, requires a certain expansion. The argumentation should be two-way argumentation, deriving consequences both from a given proposition and from its negative. Parmenides then demonstrates the method in full question–answer style, with his answerer duly responding with 'yes' and 'no'. Commentators sometimes grumble at the unconversational rôle given to Parmenides' young interlocutor. But it is one of the first rules of the eristic exercise that the answerer has, with certain exceptions, to confine himself to assent and dissent. Cornford, in his translation of the *Parmenides*, omits the

44

young Aristotle's responses, and thus obliterates the eristic procedure and intention of the dialogue. Now Zeno's own argumentation had not, apparently, taken the form of a questioner driving
an answerer into elenchus after elenchus. It had been a chain of
reductiones ad absurdum; and this is probably what Aristotle has in
mind. An eristic elenchus is, so to speak, a two-person incarnation of a *reductio ad absurdum*. But it was not Zeno who invented
this incarnation. He pitted arguments against arguments. It was
someone else who first pitted questioners against answerers. If
Zeno was the father, he was not also the mother of dialectic.

(b) *Euclides.* According to Diogenes Laertius, Euclides of
Megara studied the writings of Parmenides; his followers were
called 'Megarians', 'Eristics', and, later, 'Dialecticians' because
they put their arguments in the form of question and answer.
Euclides, we are told, rebutted demonstrations by attacking, not
their premisses (λήμματα), but their 'ἐπιφορά', which I think must
mean the inference from those premisses to their alleged conclusions. Eubulides, a follower of Euclides, is reported to have
produced many dialectical arguments in interrogative form, including the famous and important crux 'The Liar'.

Plato and other Socratics are said to have taken refuge with
Euclides at Megara after the execution of Socrates in 399. Plato
brings old Euclides into the stage-setting of his *Theaetetus*; i.e. as
still alive in 369. He is made to say that he had frequently had
conversations with Socrates on his visits from Megara to Athens.

Suidas says that Bryson, together with Euclides, introduced the
eristic dialectic.

We know very little about the Megarians, but we know enough
to satisfy us that they had very sharp noses for important logical
cruces. They consequently get short shrift from commentators on
Plato, as does Zeno, of whose earthshaking discovery of the
reductio ad absurdum the Megarians may well have been the trans-
mitters.

(c) *Protagoras.* Diogenes Laertius says that Protagoras was the
first to say that there are two opposite λόγοι about every subject;
and was also the first to argue in this way, by means of questions
(συνηρώτα). He was also the first to institute λόγων ἀγῶνας, i.e.
eristic matches or duels; he introduced the Socratic Method; and

he was the father of the whole tribe of eristical disputants. Protagoras is also reported to have written an *Art of Eristic*, and this may be hinted at in Plato's *Sophist* (232D–E). It seems to me that we have good reasons for thinking that Protagoras did introduce the exercise into Athens; and that he was the first to give coaching in its techniques and to do so for a fee. As a teacher of rhetoric, wishing to train his pupils for forensic advocacy, he might well have invented the questioner–answerer Moot. The title of his *Art of Eristic* is strong evidence for the association of Protagoras with eristic; Diogenes' explicit statements are weak evidence. But we also have ample corroboration in both Isocrates and Plato.

At the beginning of his *Against the Sophists*, which can be dated *circa* 390, Isocrates scolds the teachers who devote themselves to disputation (τῶν περὶ τὰς ἔριδας διατριβούντων). They profess to search for the truth; they promise to teach the young what to do and how to prosper; they inculcate virtue and self-control; they claim to be able to foretell the future; they charge fees which have to be deposited with a person of trust before the course of instruction begins. Now Protagoras did write a famous lecture-treatise called '*Truth*', and Plato tells us in the *Theaetetus* (178D–179A) that he claimed to foresee the future. All the rest of Isocrates' charges fit Protagoras, though maybe not only Protagoras. So Isocrates almost certainly associates Protagoras with eristic and the teaching of it. Isocrates in his *Helen* (2) again associates Protagoras with eristic.

Plato associates Protagoras with eristic in the *Protagoras*, *Theaetetus*, and *Sophist*. In the *Theaetetus* (167D–168), Socrates acting as spokesman for Protagoras, makes Protagoras say that his critics may either set up a doctrine in opposition to his own, or 'if you prefer the method of questions, ask questions; for an intelligent person ought not to reject this method, on the contrary he should choose it before all others'. He goes on to distinguish the mere match-winning eristic from the serious, truth-hunting eristic and urges his critics to pursue the latter, since familiarisation with the match-winning eristic nauseates the young with philosophy; (cf. *Rep.* 537–9, and *Phaedo* 89–90). In Plato's *Protagoras* (329B), Protagoras is described as being able to deliver a long and excellent speech, but also as able when questioned to reply briefly; and after asking a question to await and accept the answer. When Socrates at a later stage asks

Protagoras to confine himself to brief replies, Protagoras huffily says, 'I have undertaken in my time many disputation-matches (ἀγῶνα λόγων) and if I were to do what you demand and argue in just the way that my opponent (ὁ ἀντιλέγων) demanded, I should not be held superior to anyone. . . .' The expressions 'ἀγὼν λόγων' and 'ὁ ἀντιλέγων' were standard parts of the parlance of the eristic exercise. The dialogue largely consists of regulation question–answer moves, which duly result in Protagoras being driven to contradict his original thesis, but result also in Socrates' own position being turned upside-down. At one point, when Protagoras has lost his temper (337A–B), Prodicus exhorts Protagoras and Socrates 'ἀμφισβητεῖν μεν, ἐρίζειν δὲ μή' (cf. *Theaetetus* 167E–168A). Hippias urges the appointment of an umpire (ἐπιστάτης). The idea is rejected as unworthy of serious thinkers, but it is interesting as suggesting, what would *a priori* seem necessary, that at least in the students' Moots and in the exhibition bouts staged by sophists the contests may have been umpired. In the *Sophist* (225E) Plato may but need not be alluding to Protagoras, *inter alios*; at 232E, Protagoras is mentioned as the author of *Arts* of wrestling and of a lot of other things; and, since what is in question is the possibility of anyone writing an *Art* which could teach people how to dispute on any subject whatsoever, it may be that Protagoras' *Art of Eristic* is being alluded to. Though Plato thus associates Protagoras with the eristic exercise, he nowhere hints that he invented it or even introduced it into Athens. Protagoras probably died in about 411 B.C., aged seventy. So the eristic exercise must have been a familiar thing well before the last decade of the fifth century.

(d) *The Dissoi Logoi.* At the end of Diels-Kranz' *Fragmente der Vorsokratiker* there is a little piece, entitled '*Dissoi Logoi*' from a phrase occurring both in its first sentence and elsewhere in the piece. '*Dissoi Logoi*' means 'Arguments Both Ways'. The *Dissoi Logoi* is, for the most part, a sequence of theses, generally shocking ones, about each of which are marshalled first an array of arguments *pro* and then an array of arguments *contra*. Among the arguments *contra* the Thesis that *Virtue is not teachable* there is one shrewd argument which, together with an illustrative example, Plato also employs, putting it into the mouth of Protagoras in his *Protagoras* (327E–328C). This, with some corroborative evidence, strongly suggests that the backbone of the *Dissoi Logoi* derives from Protagoras himself, though some stretches, including a mention of the result of the Peloponnesian War, which was posterior to Protagoras' death, must be additions by a later hand. The whole piece is highly pemmicanised, somewhat jumbled, and fragmentary. It is written in amateurish Doric, with plenty of Ionicisms.

These arrays of *pro* and *contra* arguments seem to be designed for memorisation by students as ammunition for their questionings and answerings in eristic Moots. The piece as a whole may, therefore, have been or belonged to a primitive *Art of Eristic*. Aristotle alludes scathingly to such primitive *Arts of Eristic* at the end of his *De Sophisticis Elenchis* (183b 35–184a 10). His description of them fits the *Dissoi Logoi* well. It teaches arguments; not how to argue. At the least the *Dissoi Logoi* shows us not only that, but also in some degree how students were being trained for participation in eristic Moots before the end of the fifth century B.C. They committed to memory batches of recommended points for and against some standard theses. It is worth noticing that the author of the piece, speaking of himself as 'I', sides with the arguments *contra* the cynical or nihilist theses. Like the Socrates of Plato's Socratic dialogues, he wants the arguments *pro* and *contra* to be fairly pitted and weighed against one another, but he does not want the cynical or nihilist theses to win. He marshals the Worse and the Better Reasons, but his heart is with the Better Reasons.

(e) *The Hippocratic Writings. The Nature of Man*[1] is thought to date between 440 and 400 B.C. Its author begins by criticising some people, not physicians, who discourse on What Man is Made Of. They are eristic debaters (αὐτοῖσιν ἀντιλέγουσιν).

> Given the same debaters and the same audience, the same man never wins in the discussion three times in succession, but now one is victor, now another, now he who happens to have the most glib tongue in the face of the crowd. Yet it is right that a man who claims correct knowledge about the facts should maintain his own argument victorious always, if his knowledge be knowledge of reality and if he set it forth correctly. But in my opinion such men by their lack of understanding overthrow themselves in the words of their very discourse. . . . (Tr. W. S. H. Jones.)

[1] *Hippocrates*, Loeb Edition, vol. IV, p. 5.

This passage shows or suggests several interesting points. Eristic matches were familiar things before and perhaps well before the end of the fifth century B.C. They were conducted before audiences, and it was the audience that decided who had won. A given thesis would come up again and again for discussion, and the same debater might attack or alternatively defend the same thesis on several successive occasions. So he could and presumably would re-employ, discard, or reshape arguments that he or others had used in previous Moots. Thus we can infer that as theses were, in some measure, stock topics, the arguments for and against them would enjoy an evolution by the progressive mending of proven weaknesses. The deliberate study of the profits and losses of particular eristic tactics was possible and expedient. Two or three generations later Aristotle was to provide a theoretical basis for such study. In his *Topics* (105b 12; and 163b 17) Aristotle gives concrete tutorial advice to students on how to prepare for debates upon the themes that regularly crop up.

Against this background, the recurrence of the problem *Is Virtue Teachable?* in Plato's *Laches, Protagoras, Euthydemus, Meno,* and [*Alcibiades*] becomes explicable. It had been canvassed in the *Dissoi Logoi,* and Isocrates gives his own negative answer to it at the end of his *Against the Sophists.* There were compositions on this theme by Crito, Simon, Antisthenes, and Xenocrates. It was a constant Moot point, and consequently the arguments to it were in development. The frequent phrase 'λόγον διεξιέναι' might therefore mean 'go through a sequence of argument-moves'. Chess-players call their analogous sequences 'combinations'.

Conceivably, too, if Plato composed his early dialogues with *antilogikê* going on under his nose, then, some of their argumentative content reflects the actual argumentation of recent Moots. Perhaps these dialogues were, in part, dramatised 'documentaries' of 'combinations' recurring there.

This would explain (1) why the *Protagoras* contains a well-organised argument for the Hedonistic Calculus, though adjacent dialogues exhibit little interest in Hedonism; (2) why the *Protagoras* repeats argument-moves already made in the *Dissoi Logoi* and the *Laches.* Effective 'combinations' become stock-in-trade of the Game; (3) why these pre-*Republic* dialogues culminate not in doctrines but only in eristic checkmates. If a Moot has a finish, it ends in an elenchus.

(f) *Euthydemus and Dionysodorus*. Early in the *Euthydemus* Socrates says that the two sophists learned their brand of eristical all-in-wrestling only a year or two before the dramatic date of the dialogue, i.e. before *circa* 402 B.C. They give exhibitions of their art and also, for a fee, tuition in it. They are exponents of the match-winning eristic from which Protagoras dissociated himself. The sophist Dionysodorus may have been a pupil of Protagoras.

At 275c the lad Cleinias is described as having already had a good deal of practice in disputing (διαλέγεσθαι) and the answering of questions. This suggests that the uncorrupted eristic exercise had become popular with the young men by the last decade of the century. What was new to them was eristic prize-fighting, though they could swiftly pick up the tricks of it. In the course of the dialogue Socrates exhibits a couple of pieces of philosophically serious and edifying eristic. He does not even altogether despise the sophists' eristic tricks. He thinks that he and others ought to find out how to cope with them. Aristotle, in his *Topics*, does deal fairly carefully with a number of the 'Sotphisical Elenchi' that fill the *Euthydemus*.

(g) *Socrates*. Nearly all the specimens that we possess of eristic exercises are the elenctic question–answer operations with which, in his early dialogues, Plato credits Socrates. We have to distinguish, as commentators have not always distinguished, between, on the one hand, mere philosophical discussions; and on the other hand, the rule-governed concatenations of questions, answerable by 'yes' or 'no', which are intended to drive the answerer into self-contradiction. The latter is what should be meant by 'the Socratic Method'. Socrates himself is made to say in the *Apology* (27) 'ἐὰν ἐν τῷ εἰωθότι τρόπῳ τοὺς λόγους ποιῶμαι', before notionally driving his prosecutor into an elenchus by a duly concatenated sequence of questions. With much or little dramatic or merely conversational relief, eristic exercises dominate, or at least feature largely in *Laches*, *Lysis*, [*Alcibiades*], *Euthyphro*, *Charmides*, *Hippias Major* and *Minor*, *Protagoras*, *Ion*, *Euthydemus*, *Gorgias*, *Meno*, and *Republic I*. There is a short stretch in the *Symposium*; a little in the *Phaedo*; and the short stretch, just mentioned, in the *Apology*. The bulk of the *Cratylus* is not eristic in method, but the last twelve pages are. By contrast, there is virtually none of it in the *Crito*, in the last nine books of the *Republic*, in the *Philebus*, *Phaedrus*, or *Theaetetus*. There is no place for it in the *Timaeus* or *Critias*; or in the *Laws*, which last makes few pretences to being more than lectures. In the *Parmenides*, Part II, of course, we get our one full-scale, undramatised, even unmitigated model of a two-way eristic exercise; but here the questioner is Parmenides, not Socrates. The *Sophist* and *Politicus* are conducted not by Socrates but by the Eleatic Stranger, and he does not discuss eristically, even in the debate about the Greatest Kinds in the *Sophist*. It is interesting to speculate why a pattern of argument which had dominated the Socratic dialogues prior to Book II of the *Republic* was abandoned almost altogether from then until the *Parmenides* (II). Which Platonic Socrates are we to believe in, if either, the one who does or the one who does not employ the Socratic Method?

A propos this question, there is a curious feature of the *Theaetetus*. At the beginning and the end of the dialogue Socrates declares, almost apologetically, that his sole intellectual power is the 'maieutic' one. He can extract ideas from his answerer and test them, if necessary, to destruction. In Aristotle's parlance, he is capable only of *peirastic* cross-questioning, or what the Eleatic Stranger describes as the 'cathartic' elenchus, in the *Sophist* (230–1). Yet in his actual discussion Socrates does not handle Theaetetus as his ἀντιλέγων. Certainly some of Theaetetus' suggestions are examined and demolished, but so are some of Socrates' own suggestions and those of Protagoras who is not there to defend them. There is excellent debate, and the debate generates ἀπορίαι; but they are ἀπορίαι for Socrates as much as for Theaetetus. Save in a few very brief stretches the argumentation has not got the eristic shape or style. So we seem to be presented with an emphatic and repeated apologia for Socratic eristic accompanying a variety of philosophically admirable arguments which are not typically eristic or characteristically Socratic. The rules of the eristic Moot are almost audibly in control in, e.g., the *Protagoras*, *Euthydemus*, *Gorgias*, and *Republic* I. They are not easily, if at all, audible in the rest of the *Republic*, the *Phaedrus*, the *Theaetetus*, the *Philebus*, the *Sophist*, or the *Politicus*.

Did the real Socrates, as distinct from the Platonic Socrates of the pre-*Republic* dialogues, practise the eristic method? We do not believe Plato when he represents old Parmenides as giving a full-scale demonstration of what Aristotle's *Topics* is the *Art* of; so perhaps we should not believe Plato when he represents Socrates as repeatedly forcing elenchi by concatenations of question. Here we are without any relevant testimony from Isocrates or, surprisingly, from Diogenes Laertius; and we are without the evidence of treatise-titles. The fact that two presumably loyal Socratics, Plato and Antisthenes, both propagated the eristic technique, one in dialogues, and the other, probably, in primitive training manuals, is some evidence for their common master having taught them the use of it. When Aristotle credits Socrates with the invention of 'Induction' in his *Metaphysics* (1078b), he credits him with one of the dialectical procedures that he describes in his own *Topics*. Certainly Socratic Induction could have been used independently of eristic cross-questioning, but its incessant employment in Plato's early dialogues, and Aristotle's treatment of it as a part of dialectic suggests that it did, in fact, first live as a specifically dialectical procedure.

Subject to the debated proviso that Xenophon's ideas of the Socratic Method may all derive from Plato's dialogues, his *Memorabilia* supports the view that Socrates did practise the eristic method. Xenophon employs the semi-technical terminology of the eristic exercise in his *Memorabilia* (III. viii. 1; IV. iv. 9; IV. v. 12 to vi. 1; IV. vi. 13–15; and IV. viii. 11). I do not suppose that Xenophon understood this parlance, or that he would have recognised an elenchus if he had met one. Even more significantly, he consistently represents Socrates as asking one question after another. But, with a few exceptions, the questions are rhetorical questions, Socrates' positive views expressed in interrogative form. Their sequence does not depend on whether the answerer says 'yes' or 'no'. His interlocutor is not an adversary, and the questions do not drive him into checkmate, but merely lead him to a wiser view. It looks as if the unphilosophical Xenophon is garbling something that he has heard and misunderstood about Socrates' conduct of discussions; and this is some independent evidence that Socrates had used the Socratic Method, though independent only if Xenophon was not merely garbling the Platonic representations of Socrates at work. At least he was not plagiarising Plato.

In the slender fragments from the dialogues of Aeschines given in Chap. XI of G. C. Field's *Plato and His Contemporaries,* Socrates is represented as plying his interlocutors with chains of questions. Unlike Xenophon, Aeschines is known to have been a close associate of Socrates. Aristophanes, in the *Clouds,* certainly accuses Socrates of pitting the Worse against the Better Reason, i.e. of teaching the young men to argue as forcibly against a respectable thesis as in its favour. But this does not prove that the argumentation was of the question–answer pattern. Anyhow, Aristophanes might be pinning on to Socrates things that belonged elsewhere, e.g. to Protagoras, as he certainly pins 'physical' theories about Air on to Socrates which belonged to Diogenes of Apollonia. However, Aristophanes employs a few of the semi-technical dictions of the eristic exercise; and both the Worse Reason and Pheidippides assail their interlocutors with tail-twisting interrogations. So I think that by 423, or else by the time when he revised his *Clouds,* Aristophanes did associate Socrates with something like the Socratic Method.

If the earlier argument is allowed, that eristic was practised and taught by Protagoras, then Socrates would have been familiar with it before he was elderly. If so, then it seems likely that he would have realised at least its *peirastic* potency.

In sum, I think we are warranted in taking it that the Socratic Method was the method of the real and not only of the Platonic Socrates. We have good reason to think that he did not invent it or introduce it into Athens; but probably he improved its armoury and techniques. Possibly he emancipated it from rhetoric. But if we doubt the biographical authoritativeness of Plato's dialogues, Protagoras seems more important in the history of dialectic than was the real Socrates.

(h) *Antisthenes.* We know little about Antisthenes. He is thought, but not known, to have died, aged ninety, in about 366 B.C. He probably studied rhetoric under Gorgias, and he had pupils of his own, some of whom he took with him to sit at the feet of Socrates, i.e. before 399. His school is likely to have been, in the first instance, a school of rhetoric, since a good many of his writings appear from their titles to deal with standard rhetorical themes. What is of interest to us, however, is that his titles include 'περὶ τοῦ διαλέγεσθαι ἀντιλογικός', 'Σάθων ἤ περὶ τοῦ ἀντιλέγειν',

53

'περὶ ὀνομάτων χρήσεως ἐριστικός', 'περὶ ἐρωτήσεως καὶ ἀποκρίσεως' and 'δόξαι ἤ ἐριστικός'. All or some of these were probably training manuals, and show that the teaching of eristic, presumably as an ancillary to the teaching of rhetoric, had become an established thing well before Aristotle came to the Academy. Aristotle himself, at the end of his *De Sophisticis Elenchis*, speaks witheringly of the quality of the training manuals of eristic that his fee-taking predecessors had composed. We have no reason to suppose that he here has Antisthenes particularly in mind. I think the reference to fee-taking indicates that it is Protagoras whom he has chiefly in mind. But Aristotle's statement corroborates the impression given by the titles of Antisthenes' writings that there had for quite a long time been a market for technical instruction in eristic. Even if the training manuals that preceded Aristotle's *Topics* were merely Cram-books of *pro* and *contra* arguments, written down to be memorised by the students, and quite devoid of any general theory, still the fact of their existence shows us the pre-Aristotelian beginnings of an interest, however vocational, in the Art of elenctic argumentation. It had become a proficiency to be acquired and a subject to be studied. It had a careers-value. But it was also interesting. This interest was to develop into what we know as 'philosophy'.

(i) *Plato*. Diogenes Laertius in his *Plato* (48), confusing, as others have done, the production of dialogues with the production of dialectical arguments, says 'in my opinion Plato, who brought this form of writing to perfection, ought to be adjudged the prize for its invention as well as for its embellishment. A dialogue is a discourse consisting of question and answer on some philosophical or political subject, with due regard to the characters of the persons introduced and the choice of diction. Dialectic is the art of discourse (τέχνη λόγων) by which we either refute or establish some proposition (ἀνασκευάζομεν τι ἤ κατασκευάζομεν) by means of question and answer on the part of the interlocutors'. Later (79) he says that Plato 'was the first to frame a science for rightly asking and answering questions, having used it himself to excess'. In his *Arcesilaus* (28) he says, obviously erroneously, that Arcesilaus was the first to argue on both sides of a question (εἰς ἑκάτερον ἐπεχείρησε), and the first to meddle with the system handed down by Plato and by means of question and answer to make it more clearly resemble eristic. So it looks as if a tradition grew up according to which dialectic was a Platonic invention. I think that the word 'dialectic', with its inflections, was invented by Plato. The eristic or dialectical exercise was not invented by him, or even by his own master, Socrates. When Aristotle says that Plato's forerunners did not participate in dialectic (*Metaphysics* A 987b), he cannot mean merely that they had not got the word 'dialectic'. But Aristotle is surely here referring only to the forerunners whom he had just been describing, namely the Pythagoreans, not to Plato's forerunners in general.

III. PLATO'S DIALECTIC VIS-À-VIS ERISTIC

We have seen that what Aristotle means by 'dialectic' is just what other people meant by 'eristic', save that Aristotle is, in the main, concerned with those question–answer matches which are conducted in a pedagogically or philosophically serious spirit. But what about Plato? His accounts of dialectic in *Republic* VII, *Phaedrus*, *Philebus*, and *Sophist* give such lofty places in knowledge to the results of dialectical thinking that he seems to be talking about something entirely different from what the *Topics* is the Art of. We get the impression that in the Academy, at the same moment, the word 'dialectic' is being used in two entirely different ways, in one of which dialectic has everything, in the other nothing to do with the Moots that are held, so to speak, on Wednesday evenings between a young Coriscus and a young Theophrastus, with the not very old Aristotle or Xenocrates acting as coach, umpire, and time-keeper. I shall try to establish that for Plato, as for Aristotle, the concrete or, so to speak, Wednesday evening activity of prosecuting dialectic *is* the eristic match conducted in an academic spirit; that where Plato differs from Aristotle—and also from himself—is in his accounts of the philosophical profits of the exercise; and that even here some of Plato's accounts of these profits are not more disparate from those given by Aristotle than we should expect from our knowledge of Aristotle's addiction to logical and methodological enquiries, as well as from our knowledge of the growth and systematisation of the special sciences in the Academy.

In the *Cratylus* (390C) Socrates says, 'And the man who knows how to ask and answer questions you call a dialectician?'. In the

Meno (75C–D) he says, 'if my questioner were a professor of the eristic and contentious sort (εἰ μέν γε τῶν σοφῶν τις εἴη καὶ ἐριστικῶν τε καὶ ἀγωνιστικῶν ὁ ἐρόμενος) I should say to him: I have made my statement; if it is wrong, it is your business to examine and refute it (ἐλέγχειν). But if, like you and me on this occasion, we were friends and chose to have a discussion together, I should have to reply in some milder tone more suited to dialectic (πρᾳότερόν πως καὶ διαλεκτικώτερον). The more dialectical way, I suppose, is not merely to answer what is true, but also to make use of those points which the questioned person (ὁ ἐρωτώμενος) acknowledges that he knows.' Here we get the contrast, credited to Protagoras and constantly made by Plato and Aristotle, between the match-winning and the truth-hunting spirits in which the question-answer exercise may be conducted, with the adjective 'dialectical' used just as Aristotle uses it.

In the *Republic*, VII (534), dialectic is set up in a sovereign position over the so-called sciences. But in 537–9, we are told of the immense evil of insubordination that at present accompanies dialectic. For a young man of twenty or so, 'when met by the question What is beauty? and, having given the answer which he used to hear from the legislator, is confuted by the dialectic process (ἐξελέγχῃ ὁ λόγος); and when frequent and various defeats have forced him to believe that there is as much deformity as beauty in what he calls beauty, and that justice, goodness, and all the things which he is used to honour most are in the like predicament' he will become cynical and lawless. So only selected thirty-year-olders are to be introduced to dialectic. 'Whenever boys taste dialectic (τῶν λόγων) for the first time, they pervert it into an amusement and always employ it for purposes of contradiction, imitating in their own persons the artifices of those who study refutation (τοὺς ἐλέγχοντας) delighting, like puppies, in pulling and tearing to pieces with logic (τῷ λόγῳ) anyone who comes near them.' The senior men, however, will imitate those who are resolved to discuss and examine truth, rather than those who play at contradiction (παίζοντα καὶ ἀντιλέγοντα) for amusement. Here, too, Plato is distinguishing dialectic from match-winning eristic by the different spirits in which the same question–answer disputation exercise is conducted.

In the *Phaedo* (75C–D and cf. 78D) we hear of '. . . absolute beauty and the absolute good and the just and the holy and, in short, with all those things which we stamp with the seal of "absolute" both in our questions when we are questioners and in our answers when we are answerers.' Plato does not here use the word 'dialectic'; but he is surely referring to some regulation question–answer disputations and saying that the Theory of Forms is common to both sides in these disputations. So apparently these disputations were philosophically serious, and conformed to the pattern described by Aristotle. In the *Republic*, V (454A) Socrates distinguishes the Art of *antilogikê* from dialectic, those who employ ἔριδι from those who employ διαλέκτῳ against one another. The former are content with making empty verbal points. But both are in pursuit of τοῦ λεχθέντος τὴν ἐναντ-ίωσιν. The concrete procedure of dialectic is for Plato just what it is for Aristotle. It is the *proper* employment of the method of driving an answerer into elenchi by strategically arranged sequences of questions. See also *Philebus* (17A) and *Theaetetus* (161E).

Next, Plato and Aristotle are in complete or considerable agreement about the subordinate values of elenctic cross-questioning.

(*a*) What Aristotle calls 'peirastic' (e.g. *Topics* 169b 26) is the dialectical method as employed to prick the bubble of an individual's intellectual conceit. He thinks he knows things, but is driven to concede propositions which he recognises to be inconsistent with what he thought he knew. Plato does not use the noun *'peirastikê'*, but he and Aristotle both use the phrase 'πεῖραν λαμβάνειν' (Aristotle's *Topics*, 171b 4; Plato, *Gorgias*, 448A; *Protagoras*, 348A; *Euthydemus*, 275B; cf. *Theaetetus*, 157 C). In his *Sophist* (229–30, especially 230B–D) Plato gives a full account of how his last variety of sophist, who merits a better title than 'sophist', purges, by cross-questioning, the false conceit of knowledge. At the beginning of the *Theaetetus* (149–51D and cf. 210C) Socrates explains at length how his powers are only 'maieutic', emphasising that his kind of midwifery involvest he extinction of sham offspring.

(*b*) The *gymnastic* value of dialectic, mentioned by Aristotle (e.g. *Topics* 159a 25, 161a 25, 164a 12), is what old Parmenides gives as the reason why the young Socrates should practise the two-way Zenonian method. This training exercise is indispensable for the young man who wishes to become a philosopher (*Parmenides*, 135–6). It is an interesting fact that Socrates must be about twenty years old, just the age at which in the *Republic*, VII, Plato

E   57

had found it dangerous for people to get a taste of dialectic. Plato seems to have changed his mind. Probably dialectic practised under tutorial surveillance was proving less demoralising than he had previously feared or found. Or there may be an explanation of a quite different kind. In the *Phaedrus* Plato acknowledges, what he had denied in the *Gorgias*, that there is teachable Art of Rhetoric, but he requires that the student of it must also learn psychology and, more conjecturally, dialectic (265–6, 269E–272B, 273D–274A, 277B–C). Presumably, such a student would be of the normal age of a student of rhetoric, i.e. a young man. Even Isocrates, whose educational ideals were far from Platonic, admits the gymnastic value of astronomy, geometry, and eristic, in *Antidosis* and *Panathenaicus* (*loc. cit.*). These studies should, however, be dropped when student days are over. When he speaks of these studies as being good training for 'philosophy', he means by 'philosophy', 'rhetorical and literary culture'.

(*c*) Both Plato and Aristotle rank *agonistic* eristic low. Aristotle's strictures, however, are less wholehearted than Plato's, though even Plato now and then lets Socrates score by fairly unscrupulous argumentative tricks. Aristotle allows himself to give a good many tips in eristic gamesmanship. He is, after all, a much younger man than Plato, and probably by nature more of a controversialist. (On eristical gamesmanship see *De Sophisticis Elenchis passim*; also *Topics* 111b 12; 112a 10–15; 134a 3; 142a 32; 148a 21; 155b 25–157a 5; 158a 25–30; 159a 16–25; 163b–164b.)

(*d*) Plato and Aristotle are entirely at one in their contempt for sophistical eristic, i.e. eristic Prize-fighting.

(*e*) *The Philosophical Value of Dialectic.* First for a verbal point. When Aristotle uses the word 'philosophy', save when he speaks of First Philosophy, he normally has in mind what we mean by 'science'. Thus arithmetic, geometry, astronomy, and medicine are for Aristotle branches of philosophy. In this sense of 'philosophy' dialectic is not the whole or even a part of philosophy, though it is in important ways ancillary to scientific knowledge. Plato, on the other hand, sometimes equates the dialectician with the philosopher, as we ourselves would nowadays do; though sometimes he talks in Aristotle's idiom and treats, e.g., geometry as a branch of philosophy (*Theaetetus* 143D and *Philebus* 56D–E, 57C–D). We have recently, though only recently, come to use 'philosopher' in contrast with 'scientist', and are therefore surprised to find the Aristotelian non-equation 'dialectician ≠ philosopher'. Realisation of this partial terminological divergence of Aristotle from Plato by itself reduces a good deal the apparent gap between their views about the major value of dialectic.

Next, Plato and Aristotle agree almost completely that the dialectician's concern is with what is 'common' to, i.e. shared by and neutral between the various special branches of knowledge. He is concerned with those 'common' concepts which are ubiquitous or trans-departmental; or with those truths which are in some way presupposed by all alike of the proprietary truths of the special sciences. The concepts of *existence, non-existence, identity, difference, similarity, dissimilarity, unity,* and *plurality* are such 'common' or ubiquitous concepts (see Plato, *Theaetetus* 185–6; *Sophist* 254–9; and *Parmenides,* 136; compare Aristotle, *Metaphysics* 995b 19–26; 998b; 1004a; 1004b–1005a 18). But in the main Aristotle's emphasis is less on the ubiquitous *concepts* than on the trans-departmental *truths.* Even here, however, he has, or may have Plato with him in one of his moods; for in *Republic* VII (532–3), arguably, the 'hypotheses' of the special sciences and, presumably, the unpostulated first principle or principles are truths and not concepts. (For the trans-departmental truths with which the dialectician is concerned see Aristotle: *Topics* 101a 34–101b 4; 115b 7–15; 170a 20–170b 11; 171b 35–172b 8. *Met.* 1005a 19 et seq. *Rhet.* I. (1), 14; ii, 21; iv, 6.) Nor is there a total disparity between Aristotle's view of the rôle of dialectic *vis-à-vis* the special sciences and the view that Plato had held in *Republic* VII. True, for Aristotle the special sciences rest on their special axioms, and these departmental axioms are not the mere postulates which Plato held them to be. So for Aristotle there is no question of dialectic being a hunt for trans-departmental axioms from which the departmental principles of the special sciences will be deducible. Apparently Plato, at one time, did hold this view, though he gives us no specimens of his super-axioms. So far Aristotle does differ from Plato and, to put it bluntly, is right where Plato had been wrong. From completely topic-neutral premisses, the truths of the special sciences *could* not follow.

On the other hand, it really is the business of dialectic, according to Aristotle, to be in some way analytical or critical of the departmental axioms of the special sciences; though he does not clearly explain how or why these axioms require or benefit from such criticism. Some trans-departmental principles, which do not function as axioms, are presupposed by the special axioms of all the sciences, and the Principle of Non-Contradiction is one such principle. The establishment of such underlying and neutral principles is still eristic in pattern. (See *Met.* 1004b 15–27; 1005a 19 et seq.; 1006a 16–28; 1012a 17–28. *Topics* 101a 35–b4; 155b 10–16; 163b 8–12.) In *Met.* 1005b 7 Aristotle requires the philosopher to study, *inter alia*, the principles of syllogistic reasoning, though 'syllogistic' may here have, not the highly determinate sense that it gets in the *Prior Analytics*, but only the very broad sense that it has throughout the *Topics*. As we might put it, there are trans-departmental Formal or Logical principles presupposed by the departmental truths of the special sciences; and these logical principles need to be extracted, and can be extracted only by dialectic.

So Plato and Aristotle both credit dialectic with the task of discovering some very important trans-departmental principles which hinge on the ubiquitous, non-specialist, or 'common' concepts. They differ about the status of these principles. Plato and Aristotle are talking about the same exercise, but Aristotle is controverting an important error in what Plato had said about its philosophical proceeds. Even so, when Aristotle comes to speak of First Philosophy as the Science of Being *qua* Being, he seems to be moving nearer to Plato's position in the *Republic*.

However, in his *Phaedrus* (265–6), *Politicus* (286) and, more debatably, *Philebus* (16–18), Plato seems to give a rôle to dialectic quite different from that given in the *Republic*. We hear no more of the discovery of non-hypothetical first principles functioning as super-axioms for all the special sciences; nor is any reason given for the disappearance of this view. Perhaps daily intercourse with mathematicians, astronomers, and other researchers had taught him that no such super-axioms were to be looked for, since their absolute generality or formality would prevent special or material consequences from being derivable from them. Nor had the lack of them prevented new geometrical, astronomical, or physiological truths from being discovered. Plato, now, in the *Phaedrus*, the *Politicus*, and, debatably, the *Philebus*, seems closely to connect the task of dialectic with the tasks of Definition and especially Division, i.e. the tasks of articulating higher or more generic kinds into their lower, more specific kinds. He is tempted to treat this articulation as being necessarily dichotomous, though he prudently resists this temptation some of the time. In the *Sophist* and *Politicus* we are presented with detailed Kind-ladders, on the bottom rungs of which are the concepts of *sophist* and *statesman*. The pedagogic value of trying to build such ladders of kinds was doubtless considerable. The ideal of systematic Definition probably derives from such exercises in Division. But it is immediately clear that eristic cross-questioning cannot be the way of constructing such ladders of kinds. The answerer could not be driven into elenchus by rejection of a suggested division. Aristotle saw this (*Posterior Analytics* 91b). Nor, for that matter, does Plato make his Eleatic Stranger try to establish his divisions by eristic argumentation. A chain of *summa genera, genera, species, sub-species,* and *varieties* is not a chain of axioms, theorems, and riders. But what is more, it cannot, in general, be deductively established or established by *reductio ad absurdum*. The work of a Linnaeus cannot be done *a priori*. How could Plato, who knew exactly what question–answer arguments were really like, bring himself to say, if he did say, that the philosophically valuable results of such arguments are Kind-ladders? In the jewelled examples of the Socratic Method that fill, e.g., the *Protagoras, Gorgias,* and *Republic* I not a single Kind-ladder is or could have been established. Quite often, of course, Socrates has to draw attention to differences between different species of a genus, just as, very often, he has by means of his Induction to draw attention to their generic affinity. But until we get to the *Sophist* we have nothing reminding us of the contribution of Linnaeus to botany; nor should we have been grateful or philosophically enlightened if we had. No such divisions result out of the dialectical operations in the *Parmenides* (Part II).

Before trying to assess the claims made by Plato for Division and for Definition (in *Phaedrus* 265–6), let us consider what place is actually occupied by Division and Definition in the curriculum of the Academy. In his *Topics*, especially Book VI, Aristotle describes carefully various failings to which debaters' definitions are liable. But he does not here introduce his students to the Rules of Definition. They know them already. Similarly, in his *Rhetoric*, though he frequently employs division and constantly produces definitions, mostly very good ones, of virtues, passions, temperaments, etc., he does not have to explain what he is doing.

The so-called *Platonic Definitions* contains nearly two hundred definitions or would-be definitions. For some of the terms to be defined half a dozen or a dozen different definitions are provided. Quite a lot, though far from all of the definitions are or try to be of the Genus–Differentia pattern; and quite a lot of them embody semi-logical or semi-philosophical parlance, apparently of Aristotelian provenance. Two or three of the definitions have been culled from Plato, and eight or nine may have been culled from Aristotle. But most of the terms defined are unsophisticated terms of so little scientific or philosophical interest that any adolescent would be familiar with them; and a large number of the definitions offered are amateurish or even puerile. Over a dozen of the definitions are or closely resemble definitions which are justly demolished in the *Topics*.

It seems plausible to suppose, and I shall boldly assume, that the *Platonic Definitions* is a class album of definitions, partly culled from Plato, Aristotle, and maybe Xenocrates, etc., but mostly subscribed as beginners' essays by Aristotle's pupils themselves. To put it anachronistically, Definition was a Pass Moderations subject for freshmen in the Academy. These beginners were not yet supposed to know any science or dialectic. They were not yet even being taught rhetoric. Not one of the scores of definitions in Aristotle's *Rhetoric* has been garnered into the album, though two or three dozens of the terms defined, often very badly, in the album are terms defined, usually very well, in the *Rhetoric*.

At the end of Diogenes Laertius' *Plato*, we have ten pages of divisions, erroneously said to have been collected by Aristotle out of the works of Plato. Many, though not all of these divisions are again amateurish and even puerile attempts at the division of frequently unsophisticated and unimportant generic concepts. I take them to be specimens from a class album of divisions, i.e. a collection of, mostly, students' early essays in division assembled for tutorial criticism.

Diogenes Laertius credits Xenocrates with eight 'books' of Divisions; Aristotle with seventeen; Theophrastus with two; and Speusippus perhaps with one. Speusippus is given one 'book' of Definitions; Aristotle seven; Theophrastus three or perhaps five.

It looks to me, therefore, as if, whatever Plato promised or dreamed for Division and Definition, in mundane curricular fact they were taught to young, even very young students in the

62

Academy before they were qualified to study the Arts of Rhetoric and Dialectic—and a very sensible preliminary course this could have been. We can well imagine that the *Sophist's* half-dozen Kind-ladders terminating in the notion of *sophist*, though philosophically quite unrewarding, were intended to serve as exemplary models for the propaedeutic course on which the eighteen-year-olders were embarked. As the ladders are apparently alternatives to or rivals of one another, these could stimulate some educative comparisons and criticisms.

Similarly with the *Politicus*. Here the Stranger's voice and manner are markedly, even irksomely, those of the schoolmaster. The political concepts to which he applies his division procedures are concepts familiar to any bright lad. Save for some discussion of the notion of the Mean, the dialogue imposes no philosophical puzzles upon its recipients. It was not written to interest or profit those more senior students who were equipped to cope with the philosophical core of the *Sophist* or with either part of the *Parmenides*. Dialectic is alluded to only twice (285D and 287A), and then only in the Stranger's explanation of the preparatory rôle of the intellectual exercises that he is giving. So Plato may have composed the *Politicus* for the special benefit of the philosophically innocent novices who were at that moment getting their freshman training in the ABC of thinking. Perhaps it was the curricular needs of this special class of recipients which made Plato forget to give to the dialogue even a vestige of dramatic life.

The *Sophist* consists, queerly, of a stretch of highly abstract and sophisticated philosophical reasoning sandwiched between some division operations which presuppose no philosophical sophistication whatsoever. In the philosophical stretch, dialectic, here equated with philosophy, is described (at 253C–D), as the science which discovers how the 'Greatest Kinds' are 'joined' with and 'disjoined' from one another. Among a lot of other metaphors the term 'division' occurs once or twice. This makes it tempting to infer that Plato thought that the task of constructing Kind-ladders was not only a propaedeutic to the philosopher's or dialectician's task; it was a part of it, or the whole of it. But then we have to recognise that the Stranger's exploration of the mutual dependences and independences of the Greatest Kinds does not yield one Kind-ladder, however short. For the Greatest Kinds are not related to one another as genus to species, or as species to co-species. Aristotle seems to be saying this in *Metaphysics* III (998b). Even to render '*γένη*' by 'kinds', and *à fortiori* by 'classes', is to prejudice the interpretation of the Stranger's operations. *Existence*, *identity*, and *otherness* are not Sorts or Sets of things, embracing sub-sorts or sub-sets of things. The Stranger produces here neither dichotomous nor trichotomous divisions, for he produces no divisions at all.

In the *Parmenides* (Part II), between which and this stretch of the *Sophist* there are probable echo relations, scores of implications, real or apparent, are traced between propositions anchored in, *inter alia*, the Stranger's Greatest Kinds. But again no Kind-ladders are generated. At least Plato did not work as if he thought that his own dialectical operations were of a piece with his own exercises in division.

There is, however, one argument, besides the natural interpretation of *Phaedrus* (265–6), for the view that Plato did assimilate Division to Dialectic, namely that Aristotle does scold some unnamed person or persons for failing to see that a division is not, and is not the product of, demonstration. There need be nothing illogical in refusing to accept a recommended division (*Posterior Analytics* 91B, and cf. *De Partibus Animalium* 642b–644a). This point would assuredly not have been an obvious one in the days when Aristotle himself had not yet pre-envisaged the science of Formal Logic. So maybe Plato did fail to see that Dividing is not Reasoning and is therefore not Dialectic.

None the less, the actual propaedeutic place of division and definition in the curriculum of Plato's own Academy, together with Plato's own non-production of Kind-ladders in his *Parmenides* (Part II) and in the philosophical core of his *Sophist* itself, satisfy me that Plato knew quite well that to be good at division did not by itself amount to being good at dialectic, and so that in the *Phaedrus* passage he means but omits to say explicitly that division is only a preparation for dialectic. If this is so, then Plato, after *Republic*, VII, gives us only one statement of what kind of contribution dialectic makes to human knowledge, namely the statement in the *Sophist* (253) that dialectic reveals the mutual associations and dissociations of the Greatest Kinds. As these Kinds seem partly to coincide with what Aristotle calls the *πρῶτα γένη* (*Met.* III 998b, 999a), and with what he elsewhere calls the 'common' terms or notions, Plato's present account of the rôle of dialectic seems to have some close affinities with that of Aristotle (e.g. *Rhet.* I, II 20–22, *Met.* III 995b 21).

It is difficult to extract a hard-edged doctrine out of the metaphors in which Plato talks of those relations between the Greatest Kinds which it is the task of dialectic to disclose. But as in the *Parmenides* (Part II) old Parmenides is all the time drawing consequences, legitimately or illegitimately, from propositions that hinge on the formal or 'common' concepts, including those listed as 'Greatest Kinds' in the *Sophist*, it is possible that in the *Sophist* itself Plato is gropingly beginning to isolate for consideration such trans-departmental propositional connections as *implication, incompatibility, contradiction*, and *compatibility*. If so, then here in the *Sophist* and with fuller awareness in the *Parmenides* (Part II), he is ascribing to the dialectician enquiries which Aristotle ascribes to the dialectician, namely what we can now call 'logical' enquiries. Plato is, perhaps, adumbrating the route on which in his *Topics* lectures Aristotle is already toddling, and in his *Analytics* will before long be marching.

I say that in his *Topics* Aristotle is, as yet, only toddling, for though his purpose is to construct an Art which shall enable eristic questioners and answerers to force and rebut elenchi, he is still very unclear about the difference between (1) an argument generating an absurd conclusion because the *inference is fallacious*, and (2) an argument generating an absurd conclusion because the answerer has not noticed that at least one of the *questions* put to him was equivocal, or many questions in one, or unrestrictedly general, or metaphorical, etc. There is one and only one logical fallacy about which Aristotle is perfectly clear in the *De Sophisticis Elenchis*, namely the Fallacy of the Consequent. An answerer may erroneously think that having conceded that *if p then q*, and having also conceded *q*, he must concede *p*. But in the main, Aristotle tries to diagnose the treacherousness of arguments in terms only of internal trickinesses in their premisses. It is worth noticing that nowhere in the *Topics*, not even in the reputed Handbook of Fallacies, the *De Sophisticis Elenchis*, does Aristotle mention such formal fallacies as Undistributed Middle. His *Art of Dialectic* is not yet a work of formal logic. The *Topics* could have been taught without the Academic equivalent of a blackboard. The *Prior Analytics* could not.

Aristotle makes it a defining property of a dialectical argument that the thesis which the answerer undertakes to uphold is an 'endoxon' and not a paradox. It should be a truism, or something attested by the experts, or something obvious to the man in the street. Now, certainly, it would be a sensible piece of practical advice to a participant who wants to win an eristic duel to tell him to defend only those theses of which he and the members of the audience feel quite sure. It is much easier to think of points supporting what one believes than to think of objections to it, or to think of points supporting what one disbelieves. But Aristotle is wrong in making this a defining property of the exercise. For one thing he himself allows, what old Parmenides insists on, that the would-be philosopher should practise constructing and rebutting arguments both *pro* and *contra* each thesis and its negative. But if a thesis is an endoxon, its negative will be a paradox, so the defender of this negative will be arguing for something which he does not believe, and yet will still be operating dialectically. (See Aristotle: *Topics* 101a 34; 163b 1–15). I suspect that Aristotle overstresses the importance of the unparadoxicalness of theses for another reason. I think that his grasp of the notion of fallaciousness of reasoning is still so unsure that he is inclined to assume that a paradoxical conclusion must generally derive (validly) from something overtly or else covertly paradoxical in a premiss. The answerer must have conceded something inadvertently, so that the truism that he meant to uphold has been replaced by a paradox that he never meant to uphold.

I believe that the correct answer to the question: "What is the philosophical value of elenctic argumentation?" is much the same for both Plato and Aristotle. Both know in their bones that ἀπορίαι are the driving force of philosophical, as distinct from scientific thinking; but neither is able to state to himself why this should be so, or what sort of knowledge or insight comes from the unravelling (λύσις) of an ἀπορία. Aristotle says, with his enviable pungency, 'the resolution of a perplexity is discovery' (ἡ γὰρ λύσις τῆς ἀπορίας εὕρεσις ἐστιν) (*Nic. Eth.* 1146b 6; cf. *Met.* 995a 24–b 5); and in his practice he regularly first marshals ἀπορίαι and then moves to their λύσεις. But he never explains clearly why the person who has never been in an ἀπορία at all is to be pitied rather than envied. It is, however, not for us to complain.

66

We, too, know in our bones how philosophical problems differ in kind from scientific problems; but our statements of the differences continue to be inadequate. Wittgenstein's "fly-bottle" is the ἀπορία of the Academy. But what has the fly missed that has never got into the bottle, and therefore never looked for or found the way out of it?

CONCLUSION

Our study of the eristic or dialectical exercise has shown us something of what is going on in the Academy during the last ten or twelve years of Plato's life and the first ten or twelve years of Aristotle's teaching life. Eristic contests have become a part of the curriculum even for fairly junior members of the Academy, and both Plato and Aristotle are keenly interested not only in its gymnastic utility but also in its philosophical productiveness, in our sense of 'philosophical'. Aristotle's pedagogic interest in the Art of constructing and rebutting elenchi leads him into the pure theory of valid *versus* fallacious argument, but only at a later stage. The idea of Confutation-without-cheating precedes the idea of validity.

APPENDIX

By the time Aristotle had completed his *Topics* the eristic exercise had collected a fairly large technical and semi-technical vocabulary. Some of this vocabulary was doubtless deliberately coined by Aristotle, his colleagues and students. But a good deal of it had grown up before. We find a fairly copious vocabulary in Plato's dialogues, largely but not entirely coinciding with that of the *Topics*. I append, in no special order, the words and phrases that Plato seems to associate with elenctic cross-questioning. Nearly all of them are standard terms in Aristotle's *Topics*. ἀπορία, ἀπορεῖν, etc.; εὐπορεῖν; ἔλεγχος, ἐλέγχειν, etc.; θέσις (*Rep.* 335), τιθέναι, etc.; ὑποθέσις, etc.; λύειν, λύσις, etc.; ἐρωτᾶν, ἐρώτησις, ἐρώτημα, etc.; ἀποκρίνειν, ἀπόκρισις, etc.; ἀντιλέγειν, ἀντιλογική, etc.; ἐρίζειν, ἐριστική, etc.; ἀγών, ἀγωνιστική, etc.; διαλέγεσθαι, διαλεκτική, διαλέκτος, etc.; συλλογίζεσθαι; λόγον διεξίεναι, etc.; ἀμφισβητεῖν; συμβαίνειν; ἀκολουθεῖν; ληρεῖν (=*Ar.* ἀδολεσχεῖν); ἀδικεῖν, ἀδικία, etc.; γυμνασία etc.; πεῖραν λαμβάνειν etc.; ἐξετάζειν; φιλονικία, etc.; ἐναντία λέγειν; ἐναντίωσις; ὁμολογεῖν, ὁμολόγημα, etc.;

ἀπόδειξις; ὀνόματα θηρεύειν; ἀνατιθέναι (revoke an earlier concession); παραδέχεσθαι τόν λόγον (cf. *Topics* 159b 34); ἄτοπον; ἀπολόγημα.

Plato's phrases for the (so-called) Fallacy of Many Questions are 'δύο ἅμα με ἐρωτᾷς' and 'οὐχ ἁπλοῦν τοῦτο ἐρωτᾷς' (*Gorg.* 466C; 503A). Aristotle's regular phrase is τὸ τὰ πλέιω ἐρωτήματα ἕν ποιεῖν'.

This so-called Fallacy of Many Questions is not a fallacy at all, since it is not an argument. It is a trick-*question*. The only person who can be guilty of this foul is a questioner. The provenance of the trick was the eristic exercise. So was the provenance of the foul, miscalled the 'Fallacy', of Begging the Question, of which also only the questioner can be guilty. He begs the question, only 'begs' is a hopelessly misleading translation, when he, in effect, asks the answerer to concede the direct negative of the thesis that it is the answerer's job to defend. Even if by skilful rewording the questioner does trick the answerer into admitting the negative of his thesis, still he has not argued him into an elenchus, and *à fortiori* he has not fallaciously argued him into an elenchus.

On the whole subject of Eristic and Dialectic see:

1. G. Grote, *Aristotle* (especially Chaps. IX and X).
2. R. Robinson, *Plato's Earlier Dialectic*, O.U.P., 2nd ed., 1953.
3. E. Kapp, *Greek Foundations of Traditional Logic*, New York, 1942.
4. H. D. P. Lee, *Zeno of Elea*, C.U.P., 1936, especially pp. 113–23.

ARISTOTLE ON THE SNARES
OF ONTOLOGY
G. E. L. Owen

ARISTOTLE's commonest complaint against other philosophers is that they oversimplify. One oversimplification to which he is especially attentive is the failure to see that the same expression may have many different senses. And among such expressions there is one arch-deceiver against which he often issues warnings: the verb "to be", "*einai*". I shall discuss part of his attempt to unmask this deceiver, namely his account of the verb in what is ordinarily, and too sweepingly, called its "existential" use.

I

Aristotle often remarks that the verb "to be" has many uses, πολλαχῶς λέγεται τὸ εἶναι. Sometimes instead of the infinitive "*einai*" in this formula he writes the participial noun "*to on*", which the Oxford translators conventionally render as "being"; sometimes the same word in the plural, which the translators divorce from its singular counterpart by turning it into "things that are" or, perhaps more intelligibly, "existing things". We have to get behind these opaque translations, and an obvious first step is to collect some texts in which Aristotle draws conclusions from the verb's alleged multiplicity of use.

In *Metaphysics* A (992b 18–24) he says that because of this variety in the use of "*onta*" it is a mistake to engage in a general search for the στοιχεῖα τῶν ὄντων ("elements of *existing things*", Oxford translation). In *Metaphysics* N (1088b 35–1089b 33) he argues this thesis at length (concerning "existing things" or "things that are",

O.T.). In the *Eudemian Ethics* A (1217b 25–35) he maintains that the same multiplicity shows that there can be no single comprehensive science of *to on* ("being", O.T.). In *Metaphysics* Γ (1003a 21–b 16), resuming the same subject, he amends his claim: despite this multiplicity of use there *can* be a single comprehensive science of *to on* and *ta onta*, and those who looked for the elements of *ta onta* were very likely on the track of this science. There is a contradiction between these claims which is not our immediate business, though it is central to Aristotle's philosophical development and reflected in many other texts: I have discussed it elsewhere,[1] and it will make a brief appearance later. Our present interest in the texts is that they deal with the same topic, and that there is wide and reasonable agreement on what this topic comes to. In these contexts "being" or "*to on*" means "what there is" or "what exists". In Ross's version *Metaphysics* Γ opens with the words: "There is a science which investigates being and the attributes which belong to this in virtue of its own nature. Now this is not the same as any of the so-called special sciences; for none of these others treats universally of being as being. They cut off a part of being and investigate the attributes of this part: this is what the mathematical sciences for instance do." Ross's commentary on the passage embodies the familiar interpretation from which I want to set out. Particular sciences deal only with some part of "being", for they deal with part of what there is. Numbers are part of what there is, and mathematics deals with them; colours are another part, and mathematics does not deal with them. The same account makes sense of Aristotle's readiness to put "*to on*" into the plural and talk of a general enquiry into what there *are* (1003b 15–16), into the elements of "existing things" (1003a 28–30). Ontology is, isn't it? an accredited field of philosophy, and what Aristotle has to say of "being" in these contexts falls under ontology. If only it were so simple.

Still, this is a first, unwary step in the right direction. It steers us past an interpretation of Aristotle's words that would be proper in other contexts where he discusses the complex behaviour of the verb "to be". There is one obvious sense in which that verb, both in Greek and in English, does have many uses, but our texts

---

[1] "Logic and metaphysics in some earlier works of Aristotle", in *Aristotle and Plato in the Mid-Fourth Century*, Gothenburg, 1960, pp. 163–90: hereafter called "LM".

are not concerned with this sense. Namely, in some contexts it serves to couple subject and predicate, as it does in "Arrowby is idle"; in others it serves as an identity sign, as it does in "Arrowby is the Mayor of Margate"; in yet others it has (still provisionally speaking) the sense of "exist", as it does in "Arrowby is no more". In the *Sophist* Plato had gone some way to disentangling the first two of these uses. I do not myself think he was equally successful with the third; he seems in the end content to assimilate it to (or to scrap it in favour of) the others. That is, he treats "to be" and "not to be" alike as incomplete or elliptical expressions which always call for some completion: *to be* is just *to be something or other*.[1] And if this is so his analysis becomes the direct parent of Aristotle's.

At any rate, whatever Plato's success in the venture, it is evidently a similar broad division in the uses of the verb that Aristotle is drawing in such passages as the seventh chapter of *Metaphysics* Δ, where he marks off τὸ καθ' αὑτὸ ὄν from, among other things, τὸ κατὰ συμβεβηκὸς ὄν. But the same chapter shows that it is not these broad distinctions that he has in mind in the texts from which we set out. For he offers to take only one such general function of the verb and show that it harbours a certain multiplicity of use; and he identifies this multiplicity by saying that "being" has *different uses in different categories* (1017a 22–30). This is just what he says in our texts. In the *Eudemian Ethics*, for example, he argues that there cannot be a single comprehensive science of either "being" or "good" because these expressions signify sometimes a substance, sometimes a quality, sometimes a quantity, and so forth (1217b 25–35). So the argument in our

---

[1] Not arguable here, but the essentials are: (*a*) either "to be" or "not to be" is taken to be clarified just to the extent that the other twin is made clear (*Sophist* 250e–251a), and thereafter "not to be" is found always to need some completion (258d–e); (*b*) the idiom "partaking in being" can hardly be taken to mark off a use of the verb in which it needs no complement: see 256e and *Parmenides* 162a–b; (*c*) the contrast between *kath' hauta* and *pros heteron onta* at 255c is probably not the contrast between complete and incomplete uses of the verb but between two incomplete uses, viz. in statements of identity and of predication: this explains the *heteron* (identification does not and predication does import a complement different from the subject); it explains why the same contrast is not used a little earlier to show the difference between *identity* and being; and it explains some Aristotelian terminology (e.g. *Posterior Analytics* A 73b 5–10).

texts is confined to one general function of the verb; and this squares with the view that it is concerned with questions of existence. If the *Eudemian Ethics* is to query the possibility of any general study of *to on* in the sense of "what there is" or "what exists", it is in *this* sense that the verb "to be" must be exposed as having not one but many uses.

(Let us just notice, and shelve for later comment, the expression "*καθ' αὑτὸ ὄν*" which Aristotle uses in *Metaphysics* Δ 7 to label the relevant sense of the verb. It sounds oddly in this connection, but it comes to the same thing.)

II

Now look back at the formula by which Aristotle makes his point, *πολλαχῶς λέγεται τὸ ὄν*. For "*to on*" we shall try writing "existence" or, to mark the role of "*on*" as a grammatical predicate, "existent". Aristotle, then, is saying that "existent" has many uses. And in the *Topics* he makes it clear that to say that a word (as contrasted with a complex phrase or sentence) has many uses is to say that it is used *homonymously*.[1] Accordingly, he can remark in the *Sophistici Elenchi* (182b 13–27) that some cases of *homonymy* escape even the practised eye, and illustrate the point by a dispute over whether "being" and "one" have many uses (*ὁμωνυμίαν* . . . *πολλαχῶς λέγεσθαι*). "One" is a word whose behaviour he often compares with that of "existent": both are polygamous predicates, ready to marry subjects from any category; and "one" re-appears as a case of homonymy in *Physics* H (248b 19–21).[2] "Good" is another of this rootless family, and "good" is a prime example of homonymy in *Topics* A (107a 4–17). No doubt these are early writings; later, notably in parts of the *Metaphysics* and *Nicomachean Ethics*, he tries to improve on his earlier account. But the improvement turns out to be a sophisticated variant on the

[1] In *Topics* A 15 the multiple use of a word is *homonymy* (106a 21–2, 106b 3–4, 106b 8, 107a 5, 107a 11, 107b 7 (where the homonymy that survives *en logois* is still that of a single word, *summetrôs*), 107b 25, 107b 31): the multiple use of a phrase or sentence ("the whole *logos*", 129b 31–2, 130a 9) is distinguished from "homonymy" in 110b 16–111a 7, and illustrated under the name of "amphiboly" in 166a 6–14. (But for a deviant use of "amphiboly" cf. *Rhet.* 1407a 32, 1407a 37, 1435a 33, 1461a 26.)

[2] At 248b 19 "*εἰ ἔτυχεν*" = "*ἴσως*" (Waitz, *Organon* i 302; on such idioms, *ibid.* p. 401 and cf. Aristotle's explanation, *Topics* 156b 23–5).

idea of homonymy,[1] and it will be unintelligible if we do not follow up these older clues. We have to begin by seeing why Aristotle was inclined to class "existent" as a case of homonymy.

What he means by "homonymy" is not seriously in doubt. Commonly, though not always, he uses "homonymous" and "synonymous" to describe not words but the things to which a word is applied. Thus in the *Categories* (1a 1-11) he explains that two things (or kinds of thing) are called *syn*onymous if they both answer to some such name as "animal", and if the *logos* which corresponds to the name, i.e. the appropriate definition or paraphrase, is the same in each case. They are called *hom*onymous if both answer to the name, but the appropriate *logos* differs in the two cases. By *logos* in such contexts he plainly does mean a definition or paraphrase: this is shown by the many examples in his logic. What it is for the *logos* to correspond to the name (κατὰ τὸ ὄνομα) is not explained in the *Categories,* but elsewhere he vouchsafes that the *logos* can replace the name, that they have the same force, even that it makes no difference which one says;[2] and more cautiously that it is a necessary though not sufficient condition of the correspondence that they should mean the same.[3] (He does not state the conditions for identity of meaning.) In the sixth book of the *Topics* he tries to define the connection more rigorously. In his latest works he is still trying.

Whatever his dissatisfaction with the formal merits of his account—and it is, after all, a dissatisfaction still unassuaged in the current discussions of synonymy—it seems clear enough what is to count as a case of homonymy. "Cape" is used homonymously in English, for if I say that what I am wearing is a cape and what I am circumnavigating is a cape, I can replace "cape" at its first occurrence with "sleeveless cloak" and at its second with "point

---

[1] Which for political reasons he calls not homonymy in *Metaphysics* Γ 1003a 34 (cf. Z 1030a 34, *De Generatione et Corruptione* A 322b 31), but elsewhere not *chance* homonymy (*Nicomachean Ethics* A 1096b 26-7) or not *total* homonymy (*Eudemian Ethics* H 1236a 17): see IX below, and for details *LM* (p. 70, n. 1). Often he takes no notice of this modification of homonymy, treating homonymy as the sole complement of synonymy where single expressions are concerned (Bonitz, *Index Aristotelicus* 514a 31-40).

[2] Replacement, 21a 29, 49b 5, 101b 39-102a 1, 130a 39, 142b 3, 147b 14, 149 a 1-2; same force, 49b 3-5; no difference, 147b 13-15 (cf. 142b 2-6); all these from the logical works.

[3] 92b 26-34 and 93b 35 (cf. *Metaphysics* Z 1030a 7-9 and 1030b 7-12).

of land jutting into the sea", and these replacements are not inter-
changeable. By the rule of the *Categories* Aristotle would say that
the two things I called "cape" are homonymous; elsewhere, by a
natural shift, he would say that the word "cape" itself is homonymous.[1] We shall find this second idiom more convenient. It is
closer to English usage, and it avoids the difficulty that, on the
other way of speaking, the same things may be both synonymous
and homonymous in respect of the same word. Sea stories are a
bore in one sense, a tidal wave is a bore in more senses than
one.

(No doubt grammarians will say that in this example "bore"
is not one word but two. But the distinction did not occur to
Aristotle and brings its own snags: vide Quine, *Word and Object*,
p. 129.)

"Cape", then, is homonymous, a word with more than one
meaning. Admittedly, Aristotle's account seems too restrictive
to let in all the words that we should count as having more than
one meaning, for we are seldom prepared to identify each of a
word's meanings by finding a paraphrase for it. In some contexts
"time" can be replaced by "a term of imprisonment", but it is
notoriously less exponible in others. Yet, as though to meet this
objection, Aristotle tells us to persevere in the search for the
logos (*Topics* A 106a 1–8): it is a hard job with words such as "one"
and "being" (169a 22–5), but we shall see him engaged in it.

Here a substantial point arises. Aristotle's account of homonymy is often translated and discussed as an account of *ambiguity*.
But in the commonest use of the word "ambiguity" signifies a
very different thing from homonymy, and we shall need to hold
them apart. If we have to harden the edges of current usage a bit
in the process, there is no harm in that.

We can adapt a contrast of Mr. Strawson's and say that ambiguity shares one characteristic with truth and exaggeration which
homonymy does not share: it is a function not of expressions but
of particular utterances, the datable uses of expressions. If an
expression has more than one meaning, there need not be any
ambiguity in my words when I use it. "Bore" is homonymous in

---

[1] He is not so clear on the distinction as this suggests; but the word is
evidently the vehicle of homonymy in *Topics* A 15 (Hambruch, *Logische
Regeln*, p. 28, Lang, *Speusippus*, p. 25), as it is in *Posterior Analytics* B 99a 7 and
12, and as it seems to have been for Speusippus.

ARISTOTLE ON THE SNARES OF ONTOLOGY

English, but if I tell you "You are the greatest bore in England" you will see no saving ambiguity in what I say. On the other hand, suppose you tip the scale at twenty stone and I greet you with "You are twice the man your father was"; then what I say is ambiguous, but its ambiguity does not come from the fact that any of the expressions I utter has several meanings as "bore" has. You can, of course, accuse me of meaning more than one thing by my words, or you can ask whether I mean that you are twice as accomplished as your father or twice as heavy or whatever. But the fact that "twice" can be completed in these various ways to show my meaning does not entail that "twice" is a word with various meanings. So the occurrence of an homonymous expression is neither a sufficient nor a necessary condition of ambiguity.

This contrast deserves more space than our present purposes will allow it, but we can take it a step farther. To show that an expression has more than one meaning we must say what it means in a language; to show that an utterance is ambiguous we must say what a speaker means or might have meant by it. And the question, what I mean by my words, presupposes an answer to the question, what the words mean in the language. Typically, what I mean is a set of inferences that I intend a literate hearer to draw from my utterance; but you may miss my meaning without showing the least ignorance of the language or of the various senses carried by its homonymous words.

(Again the grammarians have their own different use for the contrast: vide Hintikka, *Inquiry* vol. ii (1959), p. 137.)

Aristotle has no word that answers exactly to "ambiguity". The closest is "amphiboly", which stands for a characteristic of a whole phrase or sentence, as "homonymy" stands for a characteristic of a particular word.[1] He does not draw the contrast between them as a contrast between words and utterances, yet some of his examples of amphiboly seem clear cases of ambiguity: witness *Sophistici Elenchi* 166a 6–7, where he draws on that rich mine of face-saving ambiguities, the Greek oracles. But he does not use the notion of amphiboly to throw light on the existential rôle or rôles of the verb "to be". He treats a statement about "the knowledge of many things" as, in effect, a case of amphiboly (*Topics* 110b 16–28), but he does not bring this device to bear on

[1] See p. 72, n. 1.

"the knowledge of existing things". He consistently regards the oddity of the verb "to be" as the oddity of one word in its context.

III

At various places Aristotle says things which show how the verb "to be" in its existential rôle or rôles can have many senses. He says in *De Anima B* (415b 13, cf. *De Gen. Corr.* 318b 25, *Eth. Nic.* 1166a 4–5) that "for living things, to be is to be alive". He generalises the point when he speaks of the "being" of a thing (its *"ousia"* or *"einai"*) as what is explicated by its definition, that is, by an account of the sort of thing it is (Bonitz, *Index Aristotelicus* 221a 41–61). And he documents it in many places, and notably in the difficult second chapter of *Metaphysics* H (1042b 15–1043a 7). Setting aside for the moment one question of interpretation, we can read the argument as follows: Some things are distinguished from others by the way their materials are put together, by blending or tying or gluing or nailing, for example; some by their position, for instance, a threshold and a lintel; some by their time, such as dinner and breakfast; and some by a combination of such marks. "Plainly, then, the word 'is' is used in a corresponding variety of ways. A threshold *is*, in that it is situated thus and so: 'to be' means its being so situated. And that ice *is* means that it is solidified in such and such a way.[1] Of some things the being will be defined by all these marks . . . e.g. hand or foot . . . For yet other things, to be is to be mixed, and not to be is the opposite. . . ."

To be, then, is always to be something or other: this comes naturally from the Greek idiom, a favourite of Plato's, which expresses "A exists" as "A is *something*". (Nor does it run counter to Aristotle's distinction in other contexts between "being something" and "simply being": vide *LM* p. 165, n. 2). It was, we

[1] Ross's account of the passage in his edition (*Metaphysics* ii, p. 228) is more correct and consistent than his translation. There is no need in 1042b 27–8 for Bonitz's τὸ κρυστάλλῳ εἶναι (an emendation which is carried farther by Jaeger's insertion in 1042b 27); this technical phrase is based on the use of the verb in predication (contrast the non-technical dative in 1042b 36 which parallels the genitive in 1042b 28 and introduces an *existential* use of the verb). τὸ κρύσταλλον εἶναι is to be understood existentially, like the comparable phrases in 1043a 2–4: that ice *is*, means that it is solid (supplying αὐτόν by analogy with αὐτό in the previous line).

conjectured, Plato's conclusion in the *Sophist*. But Aristotle is far more precise on the matter than Plato.

For one thing, while he is always ready to expand "A is" (sc. "A exists") into "A is P" for some value of "P", he rightly rejects the converse inference. It does not follow from every proposition of the form "A is P" that "A is" (*De Interpretatione* 21a 24–8), otherwise we should have to infer the existence of the non-existent merely from its being thought about (*Topics* 167a 1, 180a 32–3). For another thing he tries to meet the objection that on such an analysis of "existence" the concept of homonymy would run riot and become unworkable. It looks as though a new sense of the word will have to be conjured up for each sort of thing we want to talk about; but it is absurd to suggest that a word has not merely more than one sense but an unrestrictedly large number of senses (*Metaphysics* Γ 1006a 34–b 11). Aristotle's answer is the theory of categories. Ultimately, he holds, to be is always to be either a substance of a certain sort, or a quality of a certain sort, or a quantity of a certain sort—the list notoriously varies, but the nucleus remains stable and the number remains small (*Posterior Analytics* 83b 13–17). For these categories are the most general headings under which other classifications are grouped. And of these general headings Aristotle is ready to prove two things. First, no category is a species of any other: substances are not a kind of quality nor qualities a kind of substance (e.g. *Metaphysics* 1024b 15, 1070b 3–4). Second, no category is a species of *being* or of *what there is*, for there is no such genus as *being* (e.g. 998b 22–7). So it seems that the verb "to be" in its existential rôle enjoys a number of irreducibly different senses. Indeed, even in one category the senses of the verb will vary from one sort of subject to another, as Aristotle's examples show; but within the category the senses will have something in common which a full paraphrase will bring out. For a shark, to be is to be a *substance* of some kind; and so it is for a shamrock.[1] What Aristotle wants to dispel is the myth that there is equally something in common to sharks and shyness on the plea that each of them is a *being* or

[1] The first examples I wrote were *chalk* and *cheese*, but by Aristotle's criteria these are not strictly substances. Nor in fact are the examples quoted from *Metaphysics* H 2, as Aristotle remarks (1043a 4–5); but he adds that the argument can be transferred to substances proper. So I shall move fairly freely between the examples "ice" and "man".

existent or *thing* of some kind. There is no such genus as being (and "thing", as Berkeley confided to his notebook, is "an homonymous word").

Philosophers who remark that existence is not a predicate sometimes find support in Aristotle's argument that being is not a genus. But what Aristotle says is that "to be" means "to be so-and-so", and that the values of "so-and-so" vary with the sort of subject we assign the verb. So it seems that if Aristotle does not treat existence as a predicate this is only because he treats it as a disjunctive set of predicates. Nor is he anticipating a celebrated argument of Kant when he argues in the *Metaphysics* (1003b 27–30, 1054a 16–18) that "existent man" means no more than "man". To say that Quine is a man and exists is, perhaps, to say no more than that Quine is a man; but what assures Aristotle of this is not any conviction that "existent" is not a predicate at all, but a conviction that in this context it is a redundant predicate (*epanadiploumenon*). "Dead man" is strictly a contradiction (*De Interpretatione* 21a 21–3), and to say that Quine is not only a man but in existence is to say that he is a man and living a man's life.

What is to be said for such an analysis? It does seem to shed light on one general function of the verb "to be" which would commonly be labelled "existential". For when we say, ticking off the obituaries, that Arrowby is no more (or speak of him as no longer in existence or as having, like Wordsworth's Lucy, ceased to be), don't we mean that he no longer *lives*? Whereas, when we ask whether the rule against smoking in hall still exists, don't we mean to ask whether it is still *accepted* or *enforced*? English has an idiom that helps to mark off such existential dicta from others that will take our eye later: it lets us rephrase them with the predicate "in existence". In any language they have other marks: the predicate can be qualified by some adverbs of time—"still", "always", "no longer"—though not necessarily, as we shall see, by others; and in different contexts we call on different predicates to contradict it—"extinct", "dead", "dismantled", "disused", and so forth. According to a rule of the *Topics* (106a 12–22) this last point alone would suffice to prove the original predicate homonymous.

So Aristotle's analysis has a claim to be heard. (It is the analysis, I take it, which Mr. Geach imports to explain Aquinas' use of "*esse*";[1] and he seems content with it.) "Arrowby is no more" is a proposition in subject-predicate form. There is a first, familiar objection to this analysis: the objection is that Arrowby cannot be the logical subject of a proposition which tells us that there is no Arrowby for us to refer to. The reply, not less familiar, is that this objection confuses the reference of the name with the name's bearer. "When Mr. N. N. dies, we say that the bearer of the name dies, not that the reference dies. And it would be nonsensical to say that; for if the name ceased to have reference, it would make nonsense to say 'Mr. N. N. is dead' " (Wittgenstein, *Investigations* I, § 40). The reply has been argued more than once by Mr. Geach), and there is no need to expand it; but it leaves a residual qualm. What are the credentials, it may be asked, of a "predicate" which can continue or cease to be true of Mr. N. N., but apparently cannot come to be true of him? It makes sense to say of some individual A that A is still, or no longer, in existence; but what sense does it make to import another temporal adverb from the same class and say that A is not yet in existence? Surely this is to assume and in the same breath to deny that the name "A" has yet been given a reference? Haven't philosophers often enough vented their suspicions of the predicate in a comparable case— the alleged progress of an event from futurity to presentness or from probability to fact? But after discussion I can see little force in this difficulty. For it seems that, just to the extent that I can be said to know that some individual (say a child) will come into existence, I can be said to refer now to that individual. Certainly it is always possible that my hopeful reference will be defeated by the course of events: the child may not be born. But in this case I could not be said to know that there would be such an individual. And putative references to present or past individuals can equally be defeated by insufficient knowledge. So Aristotle's neglect of this objection seems to be neither a mark against his theory nor— what is our present concern—a difficulty for this interpretation of it. But we have other troubles of interpretation on our hands.

One such trouble is a problem that we shelved in discussing the argument of *Metaphysics* H 2. Following the natural and usual reading of that text we took it to be dealing with statements of the form "So and so exists" (p. 76, n. 1). To say of a piece of ice

---

[1] *Proceedings of the Aristotelian Society*, N.S. vol. lv (1954–5), pp. 263–4, 266–8; *Three Philosophers* (Blackwell 1961), pp. 90–2.

that it still exists is to say that it is keeping its solidity, to say that it no longer exists is to say that it has lost this solidity, i.e. melted. The notion of solidity is introduced here to give the relevant sense of "exist" (1042b 27–8). But a little later in the same chapter (1043a 7–12) Aristotle uses this same solidity to give the sense of "ice". His point now seems to be that the statement that X no longer has such solidity would be a paraphrase, or part-paraphrase, *not* of the statement "X no longer exists" (where X is our patch of ice), but of "X is no longer ice" (where X might be the water in the pond). On the whole this interest in defining classificatory words such as "ice" suits the purpose of the chapter better; but what relevance has it to the claim, made and repeated in the preceding lines, that the word "is" is used in different senses? Grant that "ice" has a different definition from "wood", how can this have the least tendency to show that when "exists" is coupled with these words it too calls for a different paraphrase?

(Here again echoes of current controversy beat in.[1] Controversy must wait its turn: at present our object is to understand.)

Let us call this the problem of the overworked paraphrase. It has connections with other resident puzzles, such as the equivocal behaviour of the words *"ousia"* and *"einai"*, which serve Aristotle both as general expressions for "being" and as special terms for the "nature" of a thing which is shown by some classificatory label and set out in its definition. We shall try first one, and then another, general solvent on such difficulties, and it will be a piece of economy (as well as a way of keeping up suspense) to raise another problem first.

This further problem is that we have presented Aristotle with an analysis of existential statements which seems to apply only, if at all, to statements about individuals which have beginnings and ends, or at least careers, in time. For suppose we want to deny in general terms that ice exists: then on such an analysis our denial becomes not empirically false but self-contradictory. It turns into "Ice is not solid" (or whatever else is taken for a defining characteristic of ice; if there are more than one, it becomes the denial that ice has at least one of these). With our particular, transient patch of ice the difficulty does not arise. To say that the ice on the pond is no longer solid, that it has melted, runs no more risk of

[1] M. White, *Towards Reunion in Philosophy*, Oxford, 1956, Chap. iv; W. V. Quine, *Word and Object*, Wiley, 1960, p. 131.

sounding like a contradiction than our report of Arrowby's death; for present purposes, the two can be taken to have the same logical form. "The ice on the pond" refers to an object, the object has melted: absurd to suggest that the reference melted with the object. But with the general proposition "Ice is not solid", the logical form seems to be not "S is not P" but "Whatever is P (or P and Q and R) is not P"; and this is a bald contradiction.

We can discount one escape route from this difficulty. It might be said: "Ice is solid, or rather frozen, water. So surely Aristotle's analysis of 'Ice does not exist' will be '*Water* is not (or, No water is) frozen', and this is no contradiction: it just happens to be false." But this cannot be Aristotle's point, for the analysis would have no tendency to show, what he plainly asserts, that for a particular subject "is" or "exists" calls for a particular paraphrase. The analysis imports another subject—Aristotle will no more confuse the water with the ice that comes from it than he will confuse the seed with the individual tree that comes into existence. So nothing in the analysis counts as the requisite paraphrase, and the homonymy of "is" remains unproven. In fact, such an analysis would be an application of the notion of amphiboly, not of homonymy at all. We must try other moves against our puzzles.

IV

The first and most obvious move is to make a virtue of necessity. Let us agree that the scope of Aristotle's analysis had better be restricted to statements about individuals and see what follows. We shall find before long that this move will not take us home, but it will bring us a long step forward.

For one thing, it seems to explain the overworked paraphrase. For suppose we set out to analyse the statement that the ice on the pond is no more: then on Aristotle's directions we shall cast around for the appropriate paraphrase of the verb "is". And to discover that paraphrase we must ask the general question, what is it to be ice? So to understand what "is" or "exists" means in our statement about the *individual* ice-patch is to understand what "ice" means *in general*. This innocuous connection seems enough to explain Aristotle's easy transition from using a certain form of words in defining a common noun such as "ice" to using the identical form of words in paraphrasing the appropriate sense of "is". If ice is frozen water, to say that any particular bit of ice has ceased to exist is to say that it has ceased to be frozen water.

From this a modicum of light is reflected on other problems. One is the ambivalent behaviour, already noted, of expressions such as *"ousia"* and *"einai"*. When Aristotle introduces *"ousia"* in the sense of the essence or definable nature of a thing, and then says that the *ousia* is, in the words of the Oxford translation, "the cause of each thing's being" (αἰτία τοῦ εἶναι ἕκαστον, *Metaphysics* H 1043a 2–3; cf. *De Anima* B 415b 12–13), he is not taking an advance draft on the Ontological Argument. He means just that the definition of "ice" goes to explain what it is for our particular ice-patch to be in existence. (To explain, not to cause: is it too late to complain of "cause" as the translation of αἰτία?)

Again, recall the expression which Aristotle uses in *Metaphysics* Δ 7 to identify that general rôle of the verb "to be" in which it carries different senses in the different categories. We took this rôle to be the (or an) existential use of the verb. Aristotle calls it τὸ καθ' αὑτὸ ὄν (1017a 7–8, 22–3), a phrase which can certainly be applied to existential statements (e.g. at *De Interpretatione* 21a 28), but which he often uses elsewhere to mark another function of the verb "to be", namely its use in definitions or in statements immediately derived from definitions. But perhaps we need not puzzle over which application of the phrase Aristotle intends in this chapter. For him it is one and the same enterprise to set up different definitions of "ice" and "wood" and to set up two different senses of "exist".[1]

Benefits flow from our restriction. Let us warm to its defence. Would Aristotle think his analysis much shaken by the fact that it makes better sense when it is restricted to the existence of individuals endowed with careers in time? Granted, it is one thing to say that the restriction clarifies the analysis, quite another to say that Aristotle saw the importance of the distinction. But doesn't he see this? He often says or implies that individuals have

[1] There are passages where Aristotle does seem to assign the *copulative* "is" a different sense in different categories: a text such as *Prior Analytics* A 48b 2–9 (cf. 49a 6–9) suggests the explanation. "A is B" can be turned into "B belongs to A", and "belongs to" has a different sense in different categories: why? Because for *red* to exist is for it to be a quality, so for *red* to belong to A is for it to be a quality of A; and the analysis would be different with predicates of substance or quantity, etc. This probably explains the odd lines 1017a 27–30 in *Metaphysics* Δ 7.

more claim than universals to be classed as ὄντα: at *Metaphysics* Λ
1071a 21–2 he says flatly that the universal Man does not exist—
particular men have particular fathers. And when he speaks of
individuals (καθ 'ἕκαστα, ἄτομα) he must not be assumed, unless the
context certifies it, to have only particular *substances* in mind. Just
as his analysis of "existence" is said to cater for all the categories,
so the line between individual and universal can apparently be
drawn in them all.[1] The distinction between a man and the species
under which he falls is paralleled in another category by the distinction between the particular, transient pallor on a man's face
and the general type of discoloration under which it falls. In
any such pair it is the first member whose existence seems to be
explained by Aristotle's analysis, just as it is the first whose claim
to be called "existent" Aristotle defends against Plato's preference
for the second. So in *Metaphysics* Λ 1070a 22–4 he says: "Health
exists just when the man is healthy. The shape of the bronze sphere
exists at just the same time as the bronze sphere. Whether anything
of it survives afterwards is another question": and by "health"
here he seems to mean just the particular state of health of the
individual.[2] For such health to exist is for it to have a temporal
career comparable with that of the ice on my pond. It is an arrangement of bodily components, and the arrangement can fall into
disrepair.

But the defence had better cool down. Already it seems to have
suggested a falsehood.

V

It has suggested a falsehood if it is taken to imply that Aristotle
wants to restrict existential statements to statements about particular men and icebergs and states of health. For of course Aristotle often makes and discusses existential statements on other
levels, statements that mention only classes or universals. In the
Posterior Analytics, for instance in A 76a 31–6 and in the opening
chapters of B, he discusses the rôle of such statements in any

---

[1] *Categories* 1a 23–1b 9, *Topics* A 103b 27–39. I can see no grounds whatever
for supposing that in the first passage an *individual* colour or piece of knowledge is one that *occurs in only one individual*. See "Inherence", *Phronesis* x
(1965) pp. 97–105.
[2] R. G. Albritton, *Journal of Philosophy* vol. liv (1957), p. 700.

systematic science. But his discussion is oddly uncertain and confused, and a particular diagnosis of the confusion seems to suggest itself.

The *Posterior Analytics* knows that being is not a genus (92b 14) and that "existing things" are parcelled into categories (88b 1–3). It is, on other grounds than the *Eudemian Ethics*, just as hostile as that work to the idea of a general science of ὄντα.[1] It holds that a logical formula which can be put to work in many fields of enquiry has a range of uses which are connected only by analogy (76a 37–40); and this might be taken to imply that "exist" has a comparable range of uses, since it can occur in such formulae. But the *Posterior Analytics* does not say that "exist" has a different sense for different kinds of subject. Instead, it draws a formal distinction between the question *whether A exists* and the question *what A is*, and even, at the start of one tangled argument, treats the second question as arising after the first has been settled (89b 34–90a 1). True, it amends this later: it contends that we can only be said to know of A's existence to the extent that we know what it is to be A (93a 21–33). Still it does not offer to paraphrase "exist" variously for different values of "A".

Here the defender of our restriction will leap in with an explanation. Aristotle's treatment of the matter here is uncertain, he will say, because Aristotle sees or half-sees that paradoxes arise if his analysis of "existence" is applied to such general existential statements as those which concern him in the *Posterior Analytics*. But this is less than half the story.

Consider the samples of existential statement that Aristotle provides in this work. They are answers to such questions as εἰ ἔστιν ἢ μή ἐστι κένταυρος ἢ θεός (89b 32): Is there a centaur? Is there a god? or, what comes to the same, Are there any centaurs, or any gods? Elsewhere he uses the concepts "straight line", "triangle", "unit of number", in similar examples (76a 34–5). So he is mentioning certain concepts and asking whether anything falls under them, or listing certain descriptions and asking whether anything answers to them.

Now such examples certainly illustrate one use of the verb "to be" which is commonly called existential: in fact, it is the use most commonly so called at present. Equally plainly it is not the rôle in which we have been watching it so far. It is the use which is

[1] Vide *LM*, p. 177.

rendered by "il y a" or "es gibt", and represented in predicate logic by the formula "(∃x) Fx". And, as that formula was designed to show, it is not in any sense a predicative use of the verb but a use which is parasitic upon all predicates. Distinguish it by two asterisks, and the use we have been discussing by one: then we can say that while Arrowby is in existence there is** at least one man still in existence, but if Arrowby dies there is** one man who is* no more. Given any form of statement in which the verb "to be" (or any other verb) plays the part of a predicate, we can construct another in which the verb "to be" takes on its non-predicative rôle. So to reconstrue this in turn as predicative would set us on a futile regress.

Aristotle nowhere distinguishes these two uses of the verb. So he is not in a position to say that his analysis of the different predicative senses of "exist" applies to being*, but not to his present concern, being**. Does this, then, explain his hesitations over existential statements in the *Posterior Analytics*?

It is the beginning of an explanation, no more. No more, because we have made our distinction look obvious (and Aristotle look something of a fool for missing it) by a gross oversimplification. We talked as though being* found a place only in statements about individuals such as the transient man or ice-patch, and being** only in statements about universals or classes; but of these propositions the second is possibly false (this is a sleeping dog that need not be woken now), and the first is certainly false. Moreover, Aristotle recognised its falsehood. Let us clear this up.

It is plain that there can be some general statements of being*. If a man can die and cease to be, a tribe can become extinct; and if a specimen of monkey can continue in existence, so, in its own way, can the species. (Certainly Aristotle does not believe in the emergence or destruction of species; but he holds that what distinguishes a species from its members is that it has a continuous career in time, *De Generatione Animalium* B 731b 31–5.) Moreover, if existence* is a predicate (or set of predicates), we can expect Aristotle to take a quite precise view of the connection between singular and general statements of existence*. In his logic, as Mrs. Kneale remarks (*The Development of Logic*, p. 63), Aristotle regards "singular and general statements as co-ordinate species of a genus. The copula and the predicate should have the same function in both." Thus the statement "Ice (still, or no longer) exists" will be related to our reports of the (continued or discontinued) existence of the ice on our pond just as the statement "Man is carnivorous" is related to our reports of this or that man's diet. For man to be a carnivorous animal, just as for Plato to be so, is for man to be an eater of meat; and for ice to be in existence, just as for our ice-patch to be so, is for it to be frozen.

Now Aristotle recognises this parallel quite expressly in the *De Interpretatione*. He marks it by writing the quantifiers "Every" and "Not every", not only in front of the harmless predicative sentence "Man is just", but in front of the *existential* sentence "Man is" (19b 15–35). Commentators for the most part skirt this fact in embarrassed silence, and if the verb "is" had to be understood here as "is**" rather than as the predicative "is*" their discomfort would be justified. For it would be absurd to write such quantifiers in front of the statement that there are** men. The quantifiers themselves must be analysed in terms of being**: to say that *every man is just* is to say that *there are** no men of whom it is not true that those men are just*, but it would be vacuous to say, and nonsense to deny, that *there are** no men of whom it is not true that there are** those men*. When the verb is understood as a predicate comparable to the predicate "is just", this bogy of absurdity is laid.

(G. E. Moore once argued that, whereas "All tame tigers growl" and "Most tame tigers growl" have a plain sense, "All tame tigers exist" and "Most tame tigers exist" do not. He was talking of being**. When he came to consider the possibility of giving the verb a predicative sense—as, for instance, when "non-existent" is taken to mean "fictional"—he qualified his thesis.)

We can take this point further. Aristotle commonly and naturally writes general statements of existence in the form "Man exists", without supplying any such prefixes as "Every" or "Not every". And if "exists" is to be understood in the second of the two ways so far distinguished (as surely it begs to be, in those examples from the *Posterior Analytics*), the omission is, as we have just seen, right and proper. But suppose it to signify being*: then the parallel between "Man exists" and "Man is just" yields a different moral. For when "Man is just" is used without any such prefix as "Every", Aristotle is ready to supply a prefix: he takes the sentence to mean "*Some* (i.e. at least one) man is just" (*Topics*

Γ 120a 6–20, *Prior Analytics* A 29a 27–9). And to say this is just to say that some statement of the form "Socrates is just" is true: "Some man . . ." promises the completion "Some man, namely Socrates . . .". By Aristotle's criteria the predicate "(is) just" will have exactly the same sense and function in these different statements, right down to the statement that begins with a proper name or some other designation of an individual.

We can expect Aristotle to apply this conclusion to "exist" in its predicative rôle; and I take him to be doing this when he says "Health exists just when the man is healthy" (*Metaphysics* Λ 1070a 22). It is not enough to reflect, as we did some pages back, that by "health" here he must mean just the particular, transient health of the individual. He is pointing a larger moral. His avowed target in the passage is Plato, and he is saying that for health to exist is not for there to be an immaterial and eternal Paradigm of Health, but just for the health of some (at least one) individual to be in existence. And for such a state of health to be in existence is, as we said earlier, for it to have a temporal career amenable to Aristotle's analysis of being*: states of health have their own ways of breaking down.

So if Aristotle can parcel out the senses of "exist" among our reports of particular cases he can fairly expect the same partitions in the use of the verb to survive in the general propositions about existence that stand on their backs. Moving from one level of generality to the other will not induce him to disentangle being* from being** but, if anything, help to blur the distinction. And thus his well-founded hesitation over the function of such a statement as "Triangle exists" in the *Posterior Analytics* will remain unresolved.

It needs no saying that the distinction he missed is a capital distinction. To predicate being*, in the appropriate sense of the word, of men or icebergs, is tacitly to presuppose that there are** men and icebergs for this predicate to apply to. Aristotle's failure to mark this difference is one, and perhaps the chief, factor in his more celebrated failure to analyse the existential presuppositions of all those forms of statement to which his system of logic applies. But such talk of "failure" makes little sense when we are mapping the advances of a pioneer.

VI

So much for our hopeful restriction on the scope of Aristotle's analysis. What remains of it? Well, it remains true, on the argument so far, that the cases of existence with which he is primarily concerned when he pigeon-holes the different senses of "exist" are particular cases, expressed in singular propositions: for we have seen how these singular propositions carry the general propositions on their backs. (Further to this see W. and M. Kneale, *The Development of Logic*, p. 31.) But having thus documented Aristotle's care for the particular, we must allow that the general propositions call for the same pattern of analysis. So the problem of the overworked paraphrase seems to be back on our hands. If ice is (*inter alia*) solid, "solid" will do double duty. It will see service not only in defining "ice" but in paraphrasing the verb "to be" when it occurs in existential statements about ice. And whatever troubles come of this will not be allayed by our artless distinction between general statements about ice and singular reports of existence which mention the ice on the pond. There are general statements of existence too, and in these the verb will call for the same paraphrase.

But by now this is the ghost of a puzzle. Our trouble with the general statement that ice exists was just that, by this double application of the paraphrase, it became a truism and its denial became a contradiction. We had no such difficulty over the statement that the ice on the pond was still, or no longer, in existence (sc. still solid or now melted). A deposed Mayor is not a Mayor, but this does not prove it a contradiction to say that the Mayor of Margate has been deposed. And now we have seen how Aristotle can assimilate the general statement of existence to the particular. "Ice exists" can be read as "Some ice is still solid, etc."; and this is no more of a tautology than the statement about a particular ice-patch which, in Aristotle's view, gives concrete filling to that general reference. In fact, our notion of generality was doubly naïve. To discover the relevant sense of "exist" in these sentences is indeed to discover what "ice" means in general; but this discovery, in its simplest form, consists in appealing not to a general statement about the ice in the world but to a definition, which is neither a particular nor a general statement about material ice but a third thing: it carries no quantifiers, and it asks not to be verified but to be understood (*Posterior Analytics* A 76b 35–77a 4).

Now notice the price to be paid for laying this ghost. We shall have to construe any assertion of existence, singular or general, as signifying that the subject is *still* in existence; and we shall have to read a denial of existence as meaning that the subject is *no longer* (or perhaps *not yet*) in existence. This suits Aristotle's observations on the existence of health and of the shape of the bronze sphere, and his query whether such things survive the perishable individual (*Metaphysics* Λ 1070a 22–4). It works well for statements about extant natural kinds and characters, such as man, or health, or ice, where statements of being** can without discomfort be replaced by, or mistaken for, statements of being*, complete with quantifiers. But when we turn to other assertions of being** it becomes absurd to rewrite "not" as "no longer" or "not yet". It is absurd to interpret "Centaurs do not exist" as referring to the dead or unborn members of some tribe. (And another example from the same context stands to refute anyone so disheartened by this that he reverts to an interpretation scouted at the end of section III. Shall we say, after all, that "Centaurs don't exist" is a statement about something in the world, namely certain "matter"; and that it says that this matter does not have the characteristics of a centaur, that flesh and blood is not horse-rumped and man-headed? Aristotle mentions gods in the same breath as centaurs, and gods have no matter at all.)

In the *Posterior Analytics* Aristotle avoids applying his analysis of being* to such statements of being**, but his avoidance never clarifies itself in a sharp distinction of the two. We offered to explain this unclarity by the consideration that *some* general statements of being** can be readily confused with statements of being*. To be sure, this consideration applies only to a range of favoured examples—to extant sorts and kinds, and classes with members; but in formal logic and philosophy and science it is these cases that preoccupy Aristotle, to the point where he is no longer concerned to resolve old uncertainties about the non-existence of centaurs or tragelaphs.

When Aristotle analyses statements of existence, in short, he is commonly preoccupied with cases of being*. But having said this we must cut the claim down to size by one last, large qualification. There is still a third kind of statement which would usually be dubbed "existential" and which plays an important part in Aristotle's argument. He seems as ready to supply a paraphrase of "existence" in these new cases as when he is dealing with men and milestones; yet it would be absurd to explain these, on the lines laid down, as cases of being*. So we need to mark off a third existential use of the verb "to be".

VII

Aristotle sometimes asserts or denies the existence of things when (*a*) the denial could not sensibly be taken to signify that the things are no longer in existence, and (*b*) the assertion could not sensibly be taken to signify that at least one sample is still in existence. Such things are time, place, the void, the subject-matter of mathematics. (It would be absurd to understand "Time exists" as signifying "At least one time, namely *now*, is still present".) Yet when he discusses the existence of the objects of mathematics he undertakes to say in detail the sense in which they can be said to exist (*Metaphysics* M 1077b 12–1078a 31). When he analyses the concept of place in the *Physics* he starts, on the recommendation of the *Posterior Analytics*, by distinguishing the question whether place exists from the question what place is, and treating the former question first (208a 28–9); but the problems he raises have the effect of making the questions coincide (209a 29–30), and the problems are accordingly lumped together as difficulties concerning the "being" or *ousia* of place (210a 12–13). He shows in what sense the existence of the void cannot be allowed (if it is equated with empty space), but also in what sense it can (as the necessary condition of motion, 217b 27–8). How are such existential claims to be taken?

Suppose I ask "Is there such a thing as centramine?" or, "as a centaur?" or, "as self-deception?" Then I may be asking, in linguistic ignorance, whether there is such a word (say "centramine") in the language. I may be asking, in ignorance of some empirical fact but knowing the use of the expression, whether anything in the world answers to the appellation (such as "centaur"). Or, thirdly, I may be showing philosophical perplexity: I may be taking for granted the ordinary use of the expression, and assuming, moreover, that its users would generally agree that something answers to it, but asking whether the accepted use of the expression (say "self-deception") is logically coherent. I am asking whether it provides a description that can be applied without generating conceptual puzzles that would justify its rejection or radical reform.

With the first of these questions Aristotle has no concern (compare Plato, who ensures that his interlocutors can at least talk Greek: *Charmides* 159a, *Meno* 82b, *First Alcibiades* 111b–c). With the second he does show concern: this is a question about being**, and "centaur" is Aristotle's example. But it is the third that is exemplified in his uncertainties over the existence of time or place or mathematicals. These uncertainties are developed in puzzles, *aporiai*, which seem to be forced on us by common beliefs (or by the contentions of other philosophers), and in particular by accredited uses of the suspect expression and other connected expressions.[1] They are consequently resolved by a clear and unparadoxical statement of what time is, or what mathematicals are. The philosophical query "Does time exist?" is answered by saying "Time is such and such" and showing the answer innocent of logical absurdities. And thus once again it becomes natural for Aristotle to speak of having shown the sense in which the subject does or does not exist (*Metaphysics* 1077b 15–17, 1078b 7–8, *Physics* 217b 27–8).

This account needs to be clarified if it is to be saved from the two major difficulties that threaten it. In the first place, it implies that to give a definition of A is tantamount to asserting that A exists: yet Aristotle himself insists elsewhere (*Posterior Analytics* B 92b 19–25) that no definition can entail the existence of what it defines. Secondly, it implies that to reject a particular definition of time is tantamount to denying the existence of time; but it is surely preposterous to think this, or to father the thought on Aristotle the codifier of dialectic.

It is not hard to see how in these contexts, and just in these, both difficulties lose their menace. The first is irrelevant because Aristotle assumes that he is analysing a concept in current use: if the notion of time can be shown to be coherent, no one (or only those with a conceptual axe to grind) will deny it application —deny, for instance, that noon today is a different time from noon yesterday. The second falls to a similar consideration. Aristotle is

[1] Vide Τιθέναι τὰ φαινόμενα, in *Aristote et les Problèmes de Méthode* (Louvain, 1961), pp. 83–103.

at pains to show that his analysis is not an arbitrary redefinition of a term. "One need not agree with the crowd in everything, but one must not desert or subvert the common and received use of words" (*Topics* Z 148b 20–2). His analysis is designed to preserve all or the most important part of common belief and usage on the subject: this explains the thorough (and supposedly exhaustive) review of the *phainomena* and *legomena* which introduces any such analysis.[1] So in a confident mood Aristotle may assume that to reject his analysis is in effect to drop the topic (indeed, to expel the topic from the language), and thus to leave the objector no means of agreeing with Aristotle's conclusion that there is such a thing.

Some may find it natural to translate Aristotle's questions in these contexts in the form "Is so and so *real*?" Certainly the verb "to be" in Aristotle does sometimes ask to be rendered by way of this slippery adjective. A contrast such as that drawn in the *Sophistici Elenchi* (170b 8–11) between "the X which *is*" and "the X which *seems*" may even suggest that when Aristotle brands the predicate "existing man" as a pleonasm (see section III above) he is thinking of what it is to be a *real* man, by contrast with some sham or half-baked or makeshift version. But this contrast would be too restricted for the context of argument. The notion of unreality has no part to play in most of the texts we have been trying to digest in this paper. If it comes in with this third kind of existential statement, it serves only to sharpen the difference between this kind and the other two.

VIII

There is no space to push this interpretation further, and not much to comment on the theory it reveals. But if we have got the general lines of it right the following observations seem pertinent.

First, there are indeed different existential uses of the verb "to be" discoverable in Aristotle's writings: we have sorted out three of these, and no doubt there are others. But Aristotle, armed only with his device for paraphrasing the predicate (and neglecting other more apt and powerful weapons in his own arsenal, such as amphiboly), gives no express recognition to these distinctions. Sometimes his uncertainties betray the cracks in the ground.

---

[1] Vide Τιθέναι τὰ φαινόμενα, in *Aristote et les Problèmes de Méthode* (Louvain, 1961), pp. 85–8.

But his own contribution to the topic lies chiefly in those distinctions which his paraphrastic technique enables him to make.

Secondly, then, where that technique is most at home, viz. in dissecting the senses of the supposed predicate being*, the credentials of the predicate are suspect. One possible source of suspicion is the equivocal status of the subject when the predicate is not yet true of it; but perhaps this suspicion was sufficiently disarmed in section III. It seems to stem from a general scepticism about our knowledge of future existence. Another trouble is an anomaly that seems to infest any negation of the predicate: but this can be settled at once. The objection is this: Let *man* be defined, after Aristotle, as an animal that travels on two legs. You ask after my man Friday, and I tell you he is no more. Then on Aristotle's analysis what I tell you is that man Friday is no longer an animal that travels on two legs; but I might have told you this if he had had, and survived, an amputation of those members. And if ice is solid by definition, still there can be crushed ice. Now this is a puzzle, not about the suggested analysis of "is" or "exists", but about the sufficient and necessary conditions for applying some classificatory word such as "man" or "ice". What the existence of crushed ice and legless men shows is that, while two legs or solidity may be a mark or characteristic of men or ice, they are not necessary conditions for applying the relevant classification—not, that is, if this would imply that "crushed ice" is a contradiction like "square circle". If such examples show anything to the purpose they show that Aristotle's view of the relation between some classificatory word and its *logos* was at one time too simple, at least if that *logos* is taken to show the conditions on which the word is correctly applied. What they do not show is that there is a looser relation between "exist" and its paraphrase in such contexts than there is between the relevant classificatory word and *its* paraphrase. If the latter is a predicate whose sense can be given in a certain form of words, so, for all that this objection shows, is "exist".

Other criticisms cut deeper. Grant that it is a different thing for a man to exist and for a sandal to exist; why should this imply that "exist" has different senses, any more than "work" must be taken to have different senses because it is one thing for a banker to do his work and another for a hangman to do his? Great numbers of words (it will be argued) are in one way or another specially

93

dependent on the context for their particular force: pronouns and demonstratives; disguised relatives like "big" and "heavy" (and even those bricks of epistemology, colour-adjectives— remember blue Persians and red cabbages); many words for working and correspondingly for idling; and many *substantive-hungry* words, to use Austin's label, such as "same", "real", "one", "good". It is not that Aristotle neglects these words: it is that he is apt, as in *Topics* A 15, to try them with the same key as words which are far less context-bound—words such as *"philein"*, which in many sentences can mean either "love" or "kiss" (106b 1–4), or *"onos"*, which can mean either "ass" or "pulley", (107a 19–21). It is just because these last expressions are relatively context-free (though notice that this freedom like others is always relative) that they are liable to generate ambiguity in use; and this is why the device of fixing their senses in advance by paraphrase is proper and valuable, and why we cannot allow them an indefinite range of senses. But we ought to be suspicious of the claim that "good" or "same" or "one" has in the same way a number of senses that must or can be listed or taught or circumscribed. Lexicographers manage to resist the suggestion. And, as Aristotle often insists, "existing" falls into the same bracket as "one" and "same" and "good".

This was a hare to be raised, not chased now. The same is true of a last questionable corollary of Aristotle's analysis, one by which he sets great store. It is that, since "exist" has many senses, there is no class of *existing things* which will embrace men and miles and modesty. The same conclusion follows from his thesis that numerals, no less than "exist", have different uses in the different categories (the fullest argument for this is *Metaphysics* I 1053b 25–1054a 19); for this entails that one substance and one quality and one quantity do not make three of anything at all. It was on this contention that he rested his rejection of any general study of what exists; and it is accordingly this thesis that he has to disarm, though not to discard, when he comes in *Metaphysics* Γ to set up his own general science of being.

Yet Aristotle is compelled to use conjunctions that his theory disallows. "Given that there are substance and quality and quantity," he starts unguardedly in the *Physics* (185a 27–8); and he comments without qualms on the restricted number of categories in the *Posterior Analytics* (83b 13–17). Nor in fact do his arguments show such conjunctions to be illegitimate, for the kind of existence that is asserted here is being**, and to this his device of paraphrasing the predicate is irrelevant. But this distinction is one of which, as we have been saying, Aristotle does not show himself aware.

IX

A final point, from abundance of caution. It may still be objected that Aristotle's account of "existent" as an homonymous predicate does not represent his most influential or characteristic view on the subject. For when he comes to set up his own general metaphysics of "being" he founds it on the claim that the different senses of "exist" in the different categories are systematically connected; and this leads him to deny that "exist" is really homonymous (*Metaphysics* Γ 1003a 33–b 19). There is a similar reconsideration in his mature ethics when he allows that "good" is after all not an instance of *chance* homonymy (*Nicomachean Ethics* A 1096b 26–7).

These developments are another story (see p. 70, n. 1). The aim of this essay, all too sketchily achieved, was to chart the basic patterns of Aristotle's analysis of existence. For that purpose it is enough to say that his later theories do not in the least entail the discarding of these patterns. His disclaimer in *Metaphysics* Γ is politic: he is announcing his own "general science of being qua being", and it was on the homonymy of "being" that he had earlier built his objection to any such enterprise. But when he now claims to detect a systematic connection between the senses of "exist" he is not denying, but presupposing, the possibility of paraphrasing that verb differently when it is married to different subjects. No doubt in claiming that these senses have something in common—that the paraphrases have an important overlap—he has moved beyond mere, or "chance", or (as the *Eudemian Ethics* puts it in another connection) "total", homonymy. But more important than these labels is the fact that his own theories were worked out wholly within the framework of those techniques on which the analysis that we have been reviewing here relies.

ARISTOTLE'S CONCEPTION
OF SUBSTANCE
D. M. MacKinnon

IN the second chapter of the fourth book of the *Metaphysics*
Aristotle considers the subject matter of metaphysical enquiry.
In the previous chapter he has identified that subject matter with
being quâ being, and he continues in the second chapter by pointing out that the term "being" is used in various senses, but with
reference to one central idea and not as merely a common epithet.
He illustrates what he has in mind by the mention of the way in
which the term "healthy" is used. If I understand aright what he
says on that subject, he argues that health of body is what may be
termed the nuclear or root-realisation of health. So we say that a
course of injections acts to restore in a body that is capable of
being restored to health, the health of which it is capable, and is
itself called healthy as efficient cause of health. Again, a habit of
daily exercise is healthy as acting to preserve the form of health
realised in the body. A complexion is healthy as a manifestation
of the health of the subject whose good health is shown by his or
her complexion. Yet injections, habits of daily exercise, complexion, health-giving, health-preserving, health-revealing though
they are, may all of them be present with the fundamental bodily
health to which they are somehow relative, absent. We may call
such a presence a counterfeit; yet we cannot deny that what we
have to do with when we meet the healthy looks of a patient in a
relatively advanced state of tuberculosis is properly and not improperly called healthy.

Where "being" is concerned, Aristotle seems to affirm an
analogous polarisation of its modes on substance. Indeed, the

metaphysician's subject matter can be, and frequently in the *Metaphysics* is, properly identified with substance as the nuclear realisation of being quâ being. Where bodily health is concerned, we do have manifestations of health, of what is properly called health, where bodily health in the full sense is absent; yet the universe of health would be without its centre, would be without its sun, if what we know as bodily health were altogether absent. It is this relation of other manifestations to the nuclear realisation of health that gives to those other manifestations what I have called their relativity. So it is with being in relation to substance.

The point is worth labouring; for it makes it clear that Aristotle's doctrine of substance belongs to his doctrine of categories. It cannot be understood except as the fundamental section of his attempt to explore the anatomy of being quâ being. To treat the theory out of context is to be sure to misunderstand what it is that in spite of subsequent philosophical history makes Aristotle's ideas continually fertile and suggestive.

Aristotle's doctrine of categories is an attempt to answer the question: what are the fundamental ways in which things are? In the fourth chapter of his work: the *Categories*, he says :

(IV.) Each uncombined word or expression means one of the following things:—what (or Substance), how large (that is, Quantity), what sort of thing (that is, Quality), related to what (or Relation), where (that is, Place), when (or Time), in what attitude (Posture, Position), how circumstanced (State or Condition), how active, what doing (or Action), how passive, what suffering (Affection). Examples, to speak but in outline, of Substance are 'man' and 'a horse', of Quantity 'two cubits long', 'three cubits in length', and the like, of Quality 'white' and 'grammatical'. Terms such as 'half', 'double', 'greater' are held to denote a Relation. 'In the market-place', 'in the Lyceum', and similar phrases mean Place, while Time is intended by phrases like 'yesterday', 'last year', and so on. 'Is lying' or 'sitting' means Posture, 'is shod' or 'is armed' means a State. 'Cuts' or 'burns', again, indicates Action, 'is cut' or 'is burnt' an Affection.

It is perfectly true that Aristotle's doctrine of categories is intended as an answer to more than one question; but it is clear that Aristotle is here attempting, whatever else he may be trying to do, some sort of inventory of the kinds of things there are in the world and the sort of relation that obtains between them. The prepositional phrase—in the world—is of course misleading; for it is at least arguable that in such a project one uses the expression "the world" as "an incomplete symbol" (in Russell's sense), requiring translation in a way less likely to suppose a readiness to treat "the world" as the proper name of some all-embracing Newtonian space. What one needs is to demand of such an inventory that it shall be exhaustive, and that it shall include as a necessary part of itself an account of the way its various constituents are related.

Now, such ontological philosophising may seem out of date, and one would be certainly hard put to it to defend the precise way in which Aristotle, in the passage quoted from the *Categories*, sets about his work. Yet ontological philosophising is still with us and, as an example of a relatively recent first-class piece of work in the field, I should like to refer to Professor Moore's well-known paper—*External and Internal Relations*.[1] The paper contains, of course, important contributions to what would now be called the philosophy of logic, especially the careful distinction between the relation between two propositions when one is said materially to imply the other, and the relation between two propositions when one is said to entail the other. But the paper is more generally concerned with a thesis developed by certain idealist philosophers, namely that the relations in which anything whatsoever enters with anything else whatsoever so affect the nature of that first thing that it would not have been the thing which it is but for those relations. Moore, very carefully and with the aid of the logical distinction between material implication and entailment which he works out, traces to its source the confusion which makes this thesis plausible. If he is successful, what he has established is something about the world. For instance, if he is right, Euler's theorem (which some pure mathematicians would regard as a discovery) might remain true and Octavius have yet been defeated at Actium and the consequent history of the Roman Principate have been quite different. What Moore establishes in this paper is something about the world, something, moreover, of a different order from the kind of facts established by the experimental and observational sciences, by historians, etc. It is a fact of a peculiar order; indeed, one is hard put to it at first, and indeed for a long time, to say clearly what sort of a fact it is. Something of the same complexity accompanies one's attempt to characterise the sort of fact that Moore in his paper succeeds in

[1] *Philosophical Studies*, Routledge and Kegan Paul, 1922, pp. 276 ff.

establishing as accompanies one's effort to understand what exactly it is that Aristotle has in mind when he speaks of being quâ being.

Enough has, however, been said to suggest that ontological enquiry is a kind of enquiry that one frequently meets in the history of philosophy. Moreover, the particular example of Moore's paper may have suggested to those familiar with the thesis it is concerned to combat and the thesis that it is concerned to maintain, that in such philosophising such notions as substance, essence, accident, relation, etc., play a conspicuously important part. Moore cannot establish against the idealists that there are genuinely contingent matters of fact, except he employ the distinction between the essential and the accidental characteristics of a thing. His use of the notions of essence and accident in the paper which I have mentioned is more conspicuous, more obvious than his use of the notion of substance; indeed, the illustration that I gave above of the consequences of his thesis might suggest that what he is dealing with is something very unlike what Aristotle has in mind when he writes of the first of his categories. Yet we shall see that where the notion of substance is concerned, part of what is fundamental to its sense is the idea of self-existence, the idea of independent existence. It is not for nothing that Aristotelian scholars find a profound influence to have been exercised on the way in which Aristotle developed his doctrine of substance by his preoccupation with criticism of the Platonic notion of *chōrismos*. Aristotle argued very strongly against Plato's doctrine of the separation of the forms; but in so arguing he carried out, in ways that sometimes one wonders if he quite consciously noticed, a logical exploration of the notion of separation which profoundly affected the way in which he saw the world; and to the way in which he saw the world the notion of substance was central. Substance is the first of the Aristotelian categories of being. Moreover, as the lengthy passage quoted from the *Categories* and the earlier reference to the *Metaphysics* IV, 2, combine to show, it is first in a very special sense. If we ask what are the most fundamental kinds of things that there are, we answer according to Aristotle that there are substances, there are qualities, etc. In the list, substance comes first because unless there are substances, there is nothing else whatever. It is not, as we saw by reference to the illustration of the predication of health, that

Aristotle denies that qualities exist; he certainly thinks that they do constitute an irreducible part of the basic furniture of the world. He is quite sure that there are qualities. Thus, if we consider the following examples, a brittle glass, a brittle china cup, a brittle stool, a brittle bone, we can distinguish the four things we have mentioned from their brittleness, which we regard as a common quality. For while brittleness is certainly a feature of many things in the world, it only exists as a feature of those things. What is substantial exists of itself; whatever else there is, whatever other fundamental modes of being there are, all are relative to substance.

Substances have qualities; they undergo changes; they suffer in respect of their qualities diminution or increase. Roses fade, acorns grow into oak trees—given substance as the focal point of our anatomisation of what there is, we can see how other modes of being are arranged in relation to it.

What has been said, although deriving from Aristotle's *Metaphysics* and *Categories*, may be thought little more than an exposition of a more or less commonsensical view of things. But what is a thing? We use the word 'thing' very loosely. We say we cannot do anything these days when we mean that our work is hopeless and that we are incapable of managing our affairs. But if someone said that an explosion was a thing, or that cleverness or stupidity were things we would be surprised and moved to protest. Cleverness and stupidity are features of our world; but this is so because there are clever and stupid men in the world, and men and women are substances as much as the brittle things I mentioned in my previous example.

Now, Aristotle, as I understand him, taught that where substances were concerned we must distinguish and recognise both primary and secondary substance. Indeed, some of the extreme difficulty that we experience in understanding his view derives from the great importance that he felt bound to give to secondary substance. What I have been thinking of up to now in this paper is primary substance; yet, as the obvious example of men and women shows clearly, primary substances demand for their articulation the essential quality which differentiates one thing from another, and renders that thing determinate. What is it that differentiates any table from any chair, any horse from any cat? Consider the latter example. Take half a dozen horses and half a dozen cats at different stages in their progress from birth to maturity. There are certain features in all of the six cats that make them cats, certain features in all of the six horses that make them horses. These are features which are the essence of the cat or the essence of the horse. They are qualities; but, according to the view now developed, we distinguish qualities which we consider essential from others which we do not so regard as essential. Of the latter some are said to belong to what they qualify *kata sumbebēkos* or as accidents. Thus if a cat is one-eyed or torn-eared, these features, however frequent, do not belong to its essence as a cat, do not belong to its substance as a cat. There are, indeed, a great many qualities characterising individual things, highly interesting to us, which do not belong to the essence of the thing. It is after all the unique features of its pet kitten which the child loves.

But if we concede this, we must acknowledge that we do in everyday life and even in the elementary stages of such sciences as botanical taxonomy[1] employ the kind of distinctions I have set out. We do suppose that there are individual things which we can group together into sorts or kinds, and we distinguish the characters that make those things the things they are from other characters which they have or acquire.

Already, however, one very serious difficulty in this ontology or account of the basic sorts of entity there are has begun to appear, and that is this. What is it that makes an individual thing an individual thing? There are very different views on this matter distinguishable in Aristotle; but for purposes of this paper I propose to reduce these conflicting doctrines to two. As my aim is less Aristotelian exegesis than an attempt to say something about ontological philosophising, the reduction or simplification is perhaps pardonable.

1. According to one of these views concerning what makes an individual thing an individual thing, the answer given identifies the individuating factor with a bare substratum, which is in fact no more than that which is qualified. As is well known, in his account of change and growth, Aristotle distinguishes four causes: material, final, formal, efficient, all at work in the process whereby acorn becomes oak tree. The last three coalesce; it is a

[1] I owe this point to Mr. J. R. Bambrough. See his paper, "Universals and Family Resemblances" (*Ar. Soc. Proc.* 1960–1).

commonplace of the commentaries to speak of final cause as formal operating *a fronte* and the efficient as formal operating *a tergo*. Formal cause is in fact essence; but reference to the other two complementing causes bestows upon this essence a dynamism which Aristotle's biological observations compelled him to emphasise. The material cause is that which is undergoing the whole process of growth, of coming to be and passing away. It is the substrate, the vehicle that bears the qualities both accidental and essential.

Now, on such a view primary substantiality is identified with the substratum element which we may say that the subject/predicate structure of our language encourages us to suppose to be there as the underlying vehicle of change and decay.

2. But on his other view Aristotle seems to recognise that this diminution of primary substantiality to the level of a bare substratum, a clothes horse on which qualities are draped,[1] is inadequate to the status he claims for the concrete self-subsistent thing that he offers us as the nuclear realisation of being. Moreover, the great pains to which he goes to show how what I have called secondary substantiality makes primary substantiality determinate, makes substances what they are, conflict with this reduction of primary substantiality to the substratum, this identification of substance with *to hupokeimenon*, almost with *sterēsis*. However, when the discussions of *Metaphysics* Γ are related to what he writes concerning transcendent substances in Λ, we have to ask whether we can suppose for one moment that he regards God, the being whose activity is defined as 'reflexive contemplation of his own contemplation', as substance in the sense of substratum. Is he not rather stressing the fact that God in a way unique among substances exists of himself? We have to reckon on this second view with an emphasis in Aristotle's enquiries whereby he seeks less to define or articulate the subject of change than to answer the question: what exists of itself? And to answer it formally by presenting as best he can the relation of the self-existent to derivative modes of existence. What is substantial on this view, what is truly individual, is the concrete thing, the determinate individual, the cat which is what *it* is, the table which is what *it* is. Here we have left far behind anything suggested by the clothes-horse image. We

[1] I owe this image, and indeed a great deal elsewhere in this paper, to my former pupil, Father Columba Ryan, O.P.

are rather concerned with concrete realisations of the features of our world that in their severalty make up that world. It is in these concretes that qualities have their indispensable setting; prised out of it they are abstract. This, indeed, is what we bring out when refusing with the nominalists to deny that they exist, we yet insist on the dependent, subordinate character of that existence.

Although the first of the two views set out derives a measure of its appeal from preoccupation with the question: what is the subject of change?—it is important to recognise that the latter view offers to this question a much more sophisticated answer. On the clothes-horse view it is the substratum which remains unaffected by the replacing of one kind of drapery by another; whereas on the latter view the concrete is itself, as concrete thing, involved in processes of change, some of which touch only what belongs to its accidental qualities, while others invade its secondary substance.

Although Aristotle's language in many places encourages the identification of primary substance with the underlying matter which is in the ultimate analysis no more than that which is informed, the *prōtē hulē*, such a view makes of primary substance a formless we-know-not-what. Le Blond in his excellent discussion of the *aporia* of substance in his book *Logique et méthode chez Aristote* points out what has been noted above, namely the absurdity of supposing God substance on such a view. He also urges as one of the prime considerations leading to such absurdity the confusion of ontological analysis, that is the attempt to present as clear as possible an inventory of the ultimate modes of being in their relation, with the quest for the ultimate subject of predication of propositions of the form: this is a such-and-such.

Suppose we ask what *this* refers to in such a proposition as: *this is King's College Chapel*; or *this is a polyanthus*; or *this is Tommy's birthday cake in the making*; or *this is typical Fenland mud*. A modern logical analyst would insist that it is the function of demonstrative or deictic symbols such as "this" to indicate as a gesture of pointing indicates, that in fact—*this is King's College Chapel*—might be rendered—*King's College Chapel—pointing*; Or: *This is Tommy's birthday cake*—by—*Tommy's birthday cake, though you mightn't think it at the moment*. But we can understand how someone reflecting on such propositions could have been led to suppose that *this* referred to whatever it was that took the shape of King's College

Chapel, the formless lump of materiality which from assuming the form of stone—(cf. *these are the stones from which the Chapel is fashioned*)—later as stone received the form of the Chapel. Yet, one has only to work out the consequences of being oneself led by such unsophisticated reflection to identify the ultimate matter with the substance, to see how impossible it is to reconcile such a view with one that gives to the substantial the ontological dignity that Aristotle certainly bestows upon it.

There are further objections to supposing that Aristotle's most mature thought could have identified the substance with the substratum in the sense of the clothes-horse, in the sense of that to which attributes are ultimately attributed. It leads, indeed, to the identification of the individuating element in the thing with something that Aristotle does not hesitate to pronounce akin to *sterēsis* or deprivation. Moreover, we have to reckon with the fact that he does in many places attribute a kind of superiority in dignity to the essential or formal element in things whether they be natural objects or artefacts; where, for instance, he stresses that knowledge is of the universal and, indeed, in the passages where he suggests almost in apologetic mood the kinship of *hulē* and *sterēsis* stressed above. In his account, moreover, of biological growth and decay which he generalises to include, e.g. the rise and fall of political institutions, while he attributes to form a final and efficient causality, denied to it by Plato, it is of the movement of form that he is writing. Yet even while he is thus drawn to exalt the formal, he is at the same time reminded that where the efficient, transeunt causality of form is concerned (and even by analogy the immanent causality manifested in growth), the finished article whether statue or building demands for its achievement the active participation of an agent who cannot be regarded as form *tout simple*, but is the necessary instrument without which form is powerless to initiate or sustain its realisation. If the stress still falls on form, it is on *embodied* form that it is laid. Thus, while in places he appears to denigrate the status of composite things, when he attends to the actualities of existence, although still regarding things as compact of matter and form and as therefore analysable into these necessarily complementary constituents (which one is tempted to regard as positive and negative poles), he is compelled to treat these concrete and existent actualities as enjoying an ontological primacy over their constituents. They constitute the substances which are first in the table of categories, but as such substances they demand for their substantiality the essential characters that make them determinate.

Enough has been said even in this grossly oversimplified sketch of the conflict of two views in Aristotle to show how subtle, how exploratory, and, indeed, how maddening his thought is. One wishes that instead of flirting with a doctrine which would depreciate the substantial to the level of a mere vehicle of characteristics, he had tightened the involved and complicated discussion that we find in the *Metaphysics* of the relations of substance, essence, and accident. There is no doubt that he is encouraged in directions exalting the formal over the concrete, leading to the near-identification of the substance of a thing with that which is grasped in its definition, by the contrast he wants to draw between substance and accident. The distinction between substance and accident is, he seems to realise, one which requires to be drawn at the level of quality rather than that of substance where substance is construed as the concrete realisation of form—the *this such*. In fact, the distinction between essence and accident drawn within the category of quality is to the modern less artificial than one drawn at the category of substance, where by the very drawing of the distinction at that point the risk seems to be run of evacuating the individual of that which makes him one rather than another— Socrates rather than Callias—through relegating the differentiating element to the status of the accidental.

Enough, however, has surely been said to show that these extremely complex discussions always inevitably arise when one essays the sort of philosophising which I have called ontological. Aristotle in the *Metaphysics* includes, under the title 'science of being quâ being', the exploration of the fundamental distinctions that we seem impelled to draw in every sort of discourse. He regards them as distinctions in that which, in respect of its underlying anatomy, has a sort of constancy. It is very hard to understand precisely how Aristotle relates the methods used in the exploration of being quâ being to the procedures followed in the Sciences, as he understands them, especially those biological sciences to which he devoted so much of his interest. Indeed, some commentators have pointed out that because he denies that being is a *genos* he cannot allow that the study of being constitutes a science in his own sense of that term. Certainly, the unity of the categories, a unity constituted by their polarisation upon sub-stance, is a unity of a very different order from that constituted by manifestation of the same specific or generic quality. Yet Aristotle was alive to the complexity of the sorts of unity we find in the world. He was all the time alert to kinds of unity too complex to be comprised under the rubrics of chance homonymity on the one side and exemplification of the same generic or specific quality on the other. His analysis of the concepts of pleasure and of pos-session are obvious examples of his sensitivity to such points. So, too, the example, worked out at the beginning of this paper, of health. Where what was fundamental in the world, where what indeed spanned the sensible and the transcendent worlds was con-cerned, this sensitivity of Aristotle to the sorts of hardly manage-able unity was at its height.

Suppose we allow that there is value in an enquiry into the sorts of entity among the enormous variety of entities that we find in the world which are the most fundamental. If one faces this question seriously, one speedily gets bogged down—and indeed Aristotle did—in its relation to other questions such as e.g. *How did things begin? What is the rationale of change and growth?* But the fact remains that we do (partly, of course, inspired by our study of logic if we are logicians) try to make inventories in which we do, however obscurely, struggle with, for example, the question of how the "thinginess' of things is related to the characteristics they have without which the things in question wouldn't be much.

Sorting things out is after all a fairly fundamental operation of intelligence. It was what Kant described as the characteristic activity of discursive understanding. It has its own widely rami-fied problems, problems incidentally, as we have mentioned, dis-cussed in many places by Aristotle with rare perception. Compare again the discussion of *having* in the last chapter of the *Categories*. It is also, of course, raised very acutely for present-day botanical taxonomists engaged in classifying different species of plant, some of which in virtue of some of their characteristics invite one identi-fication, while in virtue of others they invite another. There are sorts—we take that for granted—and by taking it for granted we advertise adherence to some principle, however elusive its formu-lation, however elastic its interpretation, that distinguishes essence from accident. Moreover, by saying that there are sorts, we say that there *are* sorts, and raise for ourselves the question of how the being of sorts is related to the being of things.

We sort out, but what is it that we sort out? What is there to be sorted out? No doubt, drawing distinctions between the existent and the non-existent, the real and the imaginary, the actual and the fictional, are sorts of sorting out. But still the assumption of a pervasive distinction, however subtle its actual realisation, between what is and what is not is not simply an admission of fundamental sorts; rather it is a distinction boded forth in the most elementary acts of affirmation and denial; there, perhaps, lies the sense of Bradley's very confused remark that reality is the ultimate subject of every judgment—judgment which Bradley understood as "the reference of an ideal content to reality". Existence, non-existence: actuality, unreality. We are here brought up against fundamental ideas distinguishable from those of essence and accident, but related to them as more fundamental. We are, in fact, brought up against the sort of consideration that led Aristotle to make substance fundamental in the universe of being.

To frame the question; what exists of itself? is to invite the categorial delineation of the manner in which other modes of being are polarised upon this centre. It is to provide a scheme of the way in which things are that cuts across, by reason of the level of abstraction to which it has penetrated, the cosmological description of the world; yet even as it cuts across that description by introducing, at a level that is ultimately not removed from the commonsensical, the crucial notion of degrees of being, it provides the instrument without which that description cannot be read aright. Aristotle's doctrine of substance is an attempt to lay the foundations of the doctrine of degrees of being at the level of the humdrum and everyday. There are distinctions within the nature of things in the most pervasive sense that we are familiar with at the point at which we ask ourselves what it is with which we have to do.

Yet the introduction at this point of a reference to the notion of degrees of being may seem surprising in view of the immediately preceding emphasis on the relevance to Aristotle's doctrine of substance of what is traditionally known as the distinction of essence from existence. It might even be thought that the notion of degrees of being stood by virtue of its mention in this place condemned again as a device whereby we conceal from ourselves the fact that in any sort of ontology we are sooner or later condemned to the mistake of preaching existence as akin to essence. But when Aristotle insisted that substance was the first of the categories, yet not altogether unlike them for all its primacy, what he was possibly trying to bring out was that the existence of things was prior to their being the things they are. Thus, in *Posterior Analytics* 2792b 13, after he had made it clear that defining man is different from affirming man to exist, he added the more general logical or ontological remark that being is in no sense essence. Yet beings are the things they are. The doctrine of the analogical unity of the fundamental modes of being, polarised upon substance, is the doctrine of the ways in which the manners in which things are are related to the fact that they are. What Aristotle does is to take the very bare notion of self-existence, of that which exists of itself, of that in which existence in contra-distinction from essence or quality is shown for what it is, and around it to group in outline, which is at once skeletal and concrete, the various modes of derivative or dependent actuality which constitute the realm of essence and of quality. To say that that which exists of itself is substance is tautology; yet it is the sort of tautology that serves to evacuate ontological analysis of the kind which Aristotle is undertaking of the charge of irrelevance in the context of enquiries very different from those which Aristotle may have conceived.

What is needed is to rescue the conception of an ontology from any sort of involvement in logical doctrines and scientific views very properly discarded. It was no accident that Collingwood in the beginning of his *Essay on Metaphysics* (1940), prepared the way for his own conception of metaphysics as a study of absolute presuppositions by criticising the view, which he said went back to Aristotle, that treated metaphysics as the science of being. It is true that in the account he gave of this alleged science of being he committed a serious mistake in that he attributed to Aristotle a view which he was careful not to attribute to him in his earlier masterpiece, *An Essay on Philosophical Method* (1933), namely, the treatment of being as a generic essence. He none the less in 1940 wanted to substitute for the study of being or ontology the critical scrutiny of successive constellations of absolute presuppositions, of fundamental assumptions which, he believed, shaped the kinds of questions we sought to put to our world, which indeed alone gave to us a world as a field for our interrogative explorations.

Leaving Collingwood's mistake aside, we see that what he is rejecting is the idea of an unconditionally valid science of the basic ways in which things are. Yet, especially if we take his *Essay on Method* into account, we can ask him whether he does not, in spite of his desire to reject ontology as incompatible with the history of science as he understands it, allow a place for some fundamental conceptual system whose anatomical structure we can see peeping through most diverse embodiments, in changing views of the way the world is. It is, I suppose, something of this sort that Quine is trying to track down in his conception of ontology as illustrated, e.g. in his essay *On What There Is*.[1] If one says that what Quine is looking for is an absolutely basic, sheerly indispensable conceptual system, the language indicates his unwillingness to commit himself to an unhesitating realism in the status which he assigns to the notions entering into that system. But one can also say that the language shows that he occupies a kind of halfway house between Collingwood and Aristotle.

For Aristotle, ontology was more than the study of the interrelations of elements in a fundamental conceptual system; for ontology was polarised upon the notion of the self-existent. One could say that for Aristotle the notion of fact was, if not consciously invoked, never far from his vision. To say that one could substitute fact for substance would be to make of Aristotle something very different from what the actual text presents to us. Yet for him the question of that which exists of itself was fundamental, showing that he was always concerned to ask what it was that our thought referred to, what indeed it was which gave direction to our thinking. The answer that he gives to this question is one that baffles the reader by its strange fusion of concreteness and extreme generality. It seems as if, in his polemic against the Platonists and elsewhere, he is always anxious to exalt the concrete over the abstract, to give primacy in being to existence over essence, so that existence is not something added to essence but that which essence requires to be shown for what it is, even if existence without specifying essence is a kind of un-being. Yet the doctrine of the categories, the characterisation of the subject-matter of meta-

[1] In *From a Logical Point of View*, Oxford, 1953.

physics as being quâ being, gives an impression of remoteness, makes one sympathetic with Collingwood's polemic for all the inaccuracy of his characterisation of the Aristotelian doctrine. We have the sense that in his view of changing absolute pre-suppositions he has his feet on the ground; whereas we may easily lose our way in trackless voids if we entertain the notion of a science of being quâ being. But, as soon as we begin to ask our-selves what, if anything, we can make of the question what it is that our thinking ultimately refers to, as soon as we pose Quine's problem of an ultimate conceptual system in more realist terms of the reference of our thought, the character of Aristotelian onto-logy begins to change, and Aristotle's doctrine of substance emerges less as the account of the essence of things which a bad historical tradition has encouraged us to find in it, than as a way of enabling us to recognise what it is for there to be a world in which distinctions obtain, within which there are many diverse things, yet related in the manner of their being one to another in ways which we can grasp.

Aristotle's doctrine of substance stands or falls with the project of ontological philosophising; yet, of course, in his own work it did not find its home simply in the bare at once formal and con-crete structure of his ontology. Reference was made earlier to the influence on his doctrine of the notion of separation and his cri-ticism of the use made of the notion by the Platonists in their doctrine of forms. For Aristotle, the notion of substance played a crucial rôle in his ontology and also in his theology; and the rela-tionship of these two, of his ontology to his theology, remains the most besettingly obscure problem in the interpretation of the *Metaphysics*. What is clear from the beginning is that the use of the notion of substance in theology is for Aristotle bound to his con-viction that substance formed the primary subject-matter of onto-logy. If his ontological analysis seems directed on the sensible world, on the world in which things are subject to change, if his very conception of things as self-existent seems suffused by his sense of the opposition of permanence to change, it is none the less true that it *is* his conviction of the possibility of ontological analysis that gives to his theology the form that it assumes. Cer-tainly, it is not irrelevant to understanding what Aristotle meant by substance, that he conceived God as substance; yet his manner of understanding the divine, of conveying the character of the divine existence, is affected by his conviction that the philosopher can lay down the ultimate forms of being, can in answering the question what thinking ultimately refers to, frame the notion of the self-existent, and around that notion and in relation to it set out the other modes of being. Aristotle's ontological work is affected by the theology of Book Λ of the *Metaphysics*; but what he says in Book Λ only begins to be intelligible, only begins to have sense to one who takes seriously the ontological project. No one can take that project seriously who does not at once differentiate existence from essence, and yet, admitting this distinction, with all its consequences, find the irreducibly distinguished existent and essential somehow related. If Aristotle's doctrine of substance is, before all else, a doctrine of the relation of the self-existent to that which is existentially derivative, it is a doctrine that also involves for its articulation such distinctions as that between essence and accident. It is not fortuitous that Moore, criticising the logical monism of the Idealists, wishing in fact to vindicate the contingent as a feature of the world, introduces the distinction between essential and accidental qualities; if he does not overtly employ the notion of substance, it is perhaps because to him the place of substance is assumed by fact. Yet fact has this in common with Aristotle's substance—that it is what is the case—it is that which exists; yet in order to be this fact and not that, it must have this character and not that.

Aristotelian scholars have devoted extensive work in recent years to determining the precise subject-matter of the *Metaphysics*. Broadly, the lines of controversy run between those who find the proper subject-matter of the *Metaphysics* in the theological topics treated in Book Λ, and those who regard ontology of the sort with which we have been concerned in this paper as the primary subject-matter of the discipline. Although the highly metaphysical flavour, in the full sense of the term, metaphysical, criticised by Kant, of the work on God encourages the modern reader to find the subject-matter of the whole work there, that section of what we know as Aristotle's metaphysics cannot easily be separated from what has gone before. It is impossible to understand at all Aristotle's conception of God without some grasp of what he means by substance. It may well be that his theology helps to rescue his ontology from the curiously ill-defined place it seems to occupy. Reference has been made to controversies among

Aristotelian specialists concerning the extent to which ontology can, in view of the analogical character of being, be regarded as a science. Certainly a modern is hard put to it to explain to himself quite how he understands the discipline. It is not a part of logic; yet it does not add to our knowledge about the world in the way in which a science is properly said to do so. It gives us a kind of insight into what is universal and familiar; it helps us to understand in ways that we have not done before the manner of the relations between the particular and the universal elements in our world. Yet we cannot regard it as a universal wisdom. We are all of us aware of the extent to which a misunderstanding of the notion of essence has hardened our intellectual arteries against the easy assimilation of evolutionary conceptions of change. Yet the kind of structure that ontological analysis suggests to us as the structure of our world seems involved in the very conception of the reference of thought to reality. Were we able, as Aristotle would seem to have been, confidently to extrapolate the crucial notion of the self-existent to the transcendent supra-sensible realm, were we at ease in positing, as he would seem to do, degrees of self-existence, almost degrees of primary substantiality analogous to the degrees of being constituted by the relation of substance to the other forms of being, we would give to our ontology the exciting quality of a kind of first step to the delineation of the relation of the world around us to its transcendent origin. But we cannot, at least without a great deal of preparation, feel confident in making this leap; yet we understand how the presence of this leap as the culmination of the metaphysical enterprise both gives to ontological analysis its excitement and also assigns to it its place. It is at once a more interesting enterprise to the generality of readers and one more easily understood if it is seen as the first step towards transcendent metaphysical statement.

Yet even if we cannot treat ontology as a kind of prolegomenon to theology in the manner of Aristotle's metaphysics the enterprise remains important, if we ask what we learn by undertaking it. It is perhaps enough to suggest that its sense and purpose shows itself. If we ask what light we gain from Moore's paper on internal and external relations, the answer that we can best give is by repeating in various ways the argument of the paper so that the importance of what we learn from it about the world shows itself.

The same would seem to be true of that sort of ontological analysis which consists in delineating the order of the fundamental modes of being in relation to the nuclear realisation of being, the primarily substantial or self-existent. The worth of what we do when we carry out ontological analysis only shows itself, and the burden of the Aristotelian notion of substance is only made clear when that notion is seen in relation to a general delineation of the modes of being of which it is the foundation, and when the worth of that delineation is itself grasped.

If this paper has shown nothing else, it may at least have made plain that the kinds of criticism of the Aristotelian conception of substance which stem from the well-known passages in Locke's *Essay On Human Understanding* dealing with the substratum, are hopelessly wide of the mark. What Aristotle is concerned with is something at once more rarefied and more abstract, and also more concrete than what Locke, in his account of the substratum in which the primary qualities of material bodies inhered, ever envisaged. Berkeley displayed a much fuller sense, in his criticism of Locke and in his own general theory, of the centrality to the notion of substance, of the conception of self-existence. When he denied that material things were substances, it is fairly clear that he was not only rejecting Locke's conception of a substratum in which primary qualities inhered, but that he was also denying that systems of actual and possible perceptions could be regarded as self-existent in the way in which he believed minds and spirits to be. Yet Locke's influence on the proper evaluation of the notion of substance in British philosophy has been disastrous. Whatever his own intentions, he has encouraged a disregard of the kind of rôle the notion fulfils in the business of ontological analysis and the sense properly attached to it when that rôle is made plain.

To speak of the notion as indispensable might be thought to give a Kantian flavour to the conclusion of this paper. The notion is, however, indispensable to ontological analysis, if one supposes that there is such an enterprise; if one says of essays within it that they are justified by the fruits of insight that they bring—then the notion possesses perhaps the only vindication that we can give it. It might be mentioned here that whatever our verdict on Aristotelian theology, the notion of substance and indeed the intellectual project of ontological analysis to which it belongs, wherein it has its home, has had a long history of use in Christian theology. To speak of ontology as having a long history of use may be thought to depart from the kind of claim made for that part of philosophy to deal with what is; but the theologian concerned to make intelligible to himself the content of his faith is by the very nature of what he assumes concerning the content of that faith encouraged to draw on the resources of a part of philosophy which, however ambiguous and elusive its subject-matter, yet seems somehow to be concerned with that which is ultimate. What we mean when we speak of concern with that which is ultimate in connection with ontology as distinct from transcendent metaphysics again must be allowed to show itself in the business of philosophising. But what made the ontological style of concern with the ultimate attractive to the Christian theologian may well have been in part that curious combination of concreteness and abstraction which we have constantly mentioned in this paper. To take one example, when Athanasius spoke of Christ as *homoousios toi Patri* he sought to bring out in the most effective way that he could the kind of identity obtaining between Christ and the Father who sent him. The student of the history of Christian doctrine is often puzzled whether the *ousia* here invoked is, in the senses which we have distinguished in this paper, *prōtē* or *deutera ousia*. The root of the difficulty, of course, lies in the uniquely close relation of the two in the kind of analysis that Aristotle undertook. We are not concerned here to ask whether Athanasius knew Aristotle; we are rather concerned with the extent to which he displayed genuine insight in invoking here in order to indicate a unique kind of identity the resources of a notion wherein the concrete of self-existence and the formal idea of essence are woven tightly together. Although primary substance, that is substance in the sense of self-existence, is prior to essence, yet without essence the self-existent lacks that which renders it determinate. One could say that when one has affirmed Christ to be of one substance with the Father, one has left altogether unresolved questions concerning the nature of the Godhead that they are affirmed to share. One has only, invoking the resources of ontology and bending them to new use, affirmed the manner of their sharing, that which is common to them, that in respect of which they are in self-existence inseparably one.

These last remarks may not properly belong to a paper whose purpose is primarily philosophical; but the notion of ontology with which this paper has been concerned is one so elusive and yet so hardly dispensable that some light on its import and indeed on its curious ambivalence of status, may be thrown from the bold use made in characteristically Christian theology of its resources. The kind of enterprise on which Aristotle embarked with a remarkable degree of sophistication and a copious amount of illuminating illustration in the *Metaphysics* may seem sterile if not nonsensical; yet we ought surely by now to be on guard against any generalised conception of philosophical method which leads us to dismiss as necessarily sterile a kind of philosophising that in spite of its uncertainty of status manifestly leads to results, manifestly enlarges our understanding of the world and of the relation of our thinking to it, makes us, indeed, more at home in the world at that point where our thought about the world and the world about which we are thinking seem to flow in to each other. It might be a paradox to say that the Aristotelian conception of substance makes us a good deal more at home with a whole number of concepts about whose sense and whose rôle in our thinking we would otherwise be deeply puzzled. Yet the notion of substance does throw a great deal of light, for instance, on the notions of things and existence. If we ask ourselves whether or not there are substances, especially if our thinking on these matters has been deeply affected by Locke's *Essay*, we find ourselves either wanting to deny that anything satisfies the conditions that Locke laid down, or else casting around in our imagination for what is suited to play the rôle. Yet it may be that these two answers to the question are both equally misguided, equally misguided because they rest on a comparable misunderstanding of what it is that ontology actually seeks to do. Certainly Aristotle was prepared to give examples of what he regarded as substantial; yet one might say that the suitability of the examples to illustrate what he sought by them to make clear must always be measured by what he shows that he is trying to set forth, and that is surely something very different from what Locke in his *Essay* is immediately concerned with. The examples Aristotle chooses he uses in contexts which make it perfectly clear that his choice of them is relative to their power in the contexts in question to thrust upon his reader's attention the notion of self-existence. The theory of substance in the form in which we find it in Aristotle stands or falls by the kind of indispensability we are prepared to allow to this notion of self-existence. We concede something of the theory if we say that a conceptual system involving the notions of self-existence, essence, etc., is hardly dispensable: we concede more if we say that it is sheerly indispensable; we concede the heart of what Aristotle is after if we say not only that it is sheerly indispensable, but that here we have to do with what is ultimate. Only if we say the last, we must remember that we are not using the term *ultimate* in ways with which later philosophising, for instance Bradleyan metaphysics, has made us familiar. The ultimacy of that with which ontology is concerned is something that, if we concede it, must be allowed to show itself. The Christian theologian who employs the notion of substance, who invokes the resources of ontology, can justify what he does by reference to the near-indispensability of the conceptual system to which they belong, to the articulation of the world of that which is. But the temper of the philosopher often encourages him to go beyond the idiom of the sheerly indispensable and boldly to say that where he is concerned with the subject-matter of ontology he touches that which is ultimate. At this point, another question shows itself, and that is the relationship of what is here called ontology to what it is fashionable today to speak of as the philosophy of logic.[1] Certainly,

---

[1] The phrase "philosophy of logic" has been introduced into philosophic parlance recently to refer to enquiries relating to fundamental notions in logic, for instance such notions as proposition, subject, predicate, relation, etc. The phrase is most commonly found in use among those who have studied deeply the work of Gottlieb Frege, and many of this philosopher's most important writings would be said to belong to "philosophy of logic". Professor G. E. Moore's very important paper on External and Internal Relations, to which reference has been made in this essay, is an excellent example of work of this kind, and many of the entries in the same philosopher's recently published *Commonplace Book* (ed. Dr. Casimir Lewy, Allen & Unwin, 1963) reflect the same sort of interest. Thus the several discussions of the relation of sentences and propositions, of tautology and contradiction (to mention only two subjects on which Moore wrote frequently) embody careful analyses of notions, fundamental in logic, and may be intelligibly said to belong to its philosophy.

There is, however, need to clarify the precise relations between philosophy of logic and some of the work conventionally called epistemological and also its differences from the enquiries called ontological with which this essay has been concerned, and which are themselves various in scope and

those who prefer the more modest idiom of a sheerly indispensable conceptual system to the bolder claims to be concerned with that which is ultimate, are for the most part prepared to concede to the discipline, commonly called the theory of knowledge, a very important part in the body of philosophy. Some of those who speak most often of the philosophy of logic are also anxious to dispute the claim of the theory of knowledge to this pre-eminence —even if some of the things which they claim for philosophy of logic seem curiously like what has in the past been regarded as among the tasks of the theory of knowledge. But it may be that those who speak of philosophy of logic prefer this language as less tainted with the sort of subjectivism which some have discerned even in so acute and comprehensive and so critical a philosopher as Kant, a subjectivism that affects his understanding of categories, encouraging him to deploy a system of categories of understanding rather than categories of being. The Aristotelian categories, however much the list may have been affected by Aristotle's concentration upon the sensible world whose laws were laws of change and decay, are categories of being. They are ways in which things are; they are more than indispensable forms of representation; they are those fundamental modes of being which we are compelled to affirm in acknowledgment of the reference of thought to that to which it is evidently directed.

A full reconsideration of the Aristotelian conception of substance must issue in raising in a new way the perennially recurrent philosophical disputes between realism and subjectivism. Those who claim for ontology a genuine concern with the ultimate are in the very making of this claim committing themselves to one of the most important insights characteristic of the realist. Moreover, when one comes to see that the insight of the realist is something which we grasp by attention to the Aristotelian doctrine of categories, we come to see that insight itself in a new way, in a way that is liberated from an over-preoccupation with problems relating to the status and nature of objects of perception.

Although, therefore, the precise standing of ontology remains obscure, it is fairly evident that engagement with its problems,

intention, including both Aristotle's anatomisation of being and Mr. P. F. Strawson's "descriptive metaphysics", as defined and illustrated in his book: *Individuals* (Methuen, 1959).

engagement, that is, with the issues raised by the Aristotelian conception of substance, brings one at once up against absolutely central issues in philosophy, enabling one also to transform some of these issues into new shapes and so transforming them at once gain insight concerning what is at issue in them and also advance some way to their solution.

ARISTOTLE'S DISTINCTION
BETWEEN
ENERGEIA AND *KINESIS*
J. L. Ackrill

I. INTRODUCTION

IN *Metaphysics* Θ 6 Aristotle first gives a general explanation of the notion of *energeia* as opposed to *dunamis*—actuality as opposed to potentiality. He then draws a distinction between *energeia* and *kinesis*. '*Kinesis*' is Aristotle's regular word for change, including movement. *Kinesis* is itself an *energeia* in the wide sense, an actuality as opposed to a potentiality. So in distinguishing it from *energeia* Aristotle is evidently using '*energeia*' in a new and narrower sense. This distinction between *energeia* and *kinesis* occurs in a number of places in Aristotle, and the commentators seem to be fairly happy about it. Yet it is not easy to understand precisely what distinction Aristotle has in mind.

There are several reasons why the distinction between *energeia* and *kinesis* is worth studying. (*a*) It crops up, as will be seen, in a variety of important contexts in Aristotle. (*b*) It is closely related to the distinction between action (πρᾶξις) and production (ποίησις) which plays a leading part in Aristotle's ethical writings. (*c*) The difficulties we encounter in trying to give a clear and consistent interpretation of what Aristotle says about *energeia* and *kinesis* are largely due to features of his thought and writing which cause equal trouble in other parts of his philosophy; so that to diagnose these features in this relatively limited area would be a help towards explaining his treatment of quite other topics. (*d*) The point or points that Aristotle is trying to bring out with this distinction are of continuing philosophical interest.

This paper is primarily aporetic and destructive. Some of the relevant passages are examined, and some difficulties are raised. The aim is to stimulate, not to close, discussion of the problems.

The words '*energeia*' and '*kinesis*' will be left untranslated and, from now on, unitalicised. The word 'activities' will be used, where convenient, to cover both energeiai and kineseis; this is not to imply that the performances, operations, etc., which are in question would all be naturally described in English as 'activities'.

II. METAPHYSICS Θ 6

The passage on energeia and kinesis, 1048b 18–35, divides into two parts. Aristotle first speaks of actions (πράξεις), and distinguishes between those that are 'perfect' (τελείαι) and those that are not. Some actions have a limit (πέρας), others do not. An action that has a limit is not itself an end (τέλος) but is directed to an end or goal (οὗ ἕνεκα) which is not yet in existence during the course of the action. Such an action is not perfect. On the other hand, an action that has no limit is one which is an end, or one in which the end is present (ἐνυπάρχει τὸ τέλος); this is a perfect action. Aristotle now passes to remarks evidently intended to elucidate the foregoing distinction. In these remarks (1048b 23–35) he distinguishes between energeiai and kineseis by the repeated use of formulae which combine present tenses with perfect tenses. Thus he starts: 'at the same time one sees [or "is seeing"—there is no distinct continuous present in Greek] and has seen, understands and has understood, thinks and has thought; while it is not true that at the same time one learns and has learnt or is being cured and has been cured'. So seeing, understanding, and thinking are energeiai, learning and being cured are kineseis. Among other examples he uses here are (for energeiai) living well and being happy, (for kineseis) walking and house-building.

What exactly is the force of Aristotle's point about present and perfect tenses? The earlier distinction between activities which have a limit and those which have not naturally suggests the distinction between activities which are indefinitely continuable and those which are not: I cannot go on building a house once I have built it, but I can go on thinking of something though it is already true to say that I have thought of it. This is certainly one thing that Aristotle means to bring out by his present and perfect tense formulae. For after saying 'at the same time one is living well and has lived well, and is happy and has been happy' he goes on: 'otherwise it would have to stop at some time'. Thus he takes the propriety or impropriety of combining present and perfect tenses as tied to the possibility or impossibility of going on with the activity indefinitely. And when he continues: 'but in fact it is not [*scilicet*, necessary for it to stop at some time], but one lives and has lived', one naturally understands these last words to mean that a man can go on living though he has already lived. Perhaps this is the only point that Aristotle is making with his presents and perfects, the point, namely, that with some activities X the moment at which one can say 'he has Xed' necessarily terminates the period of Xing, while with other activities Y there is no absurdity in saying that a man is still going on Ying even though it would already be true to say 'he has Yed'.

Quite a different point has, however, often been read into Aristotle's 'at the same time one sees and has seen'. It has been taken as saying (not, or not only, that 'one sees' does not exclude 'one has seen', but) that whenever 'one sees' is true so also is 'one has seen', that is, that 'sees' *entails* 'has seen'; similarly, of course, for all the other energeia-verbs. Thus Sir David Ross, in the Introduction to his edition of the *Metaphysics* (Oxford, 1924, p. cxxviii), says that an energeia 'is complete in each moment of it-self; at the same moment you see and have seen, know and have known'. Professor Ryle, in *Dilemmas* (Cambridge, 1954, p. 102), says that in our passage Aristotle points out that you can say 'I have seen' as soon as you can say 'I see'.

Now it seems highly doubtful whether this *is* pointed out in our passage. Anyone, I suppose, will understand 'it is not true that at the same time one learns and has learnt' as meaning—*not* that 'learns' does not *entail* 'has learnt' but—that 'learns' and 'has learnt' are *incompatible*. Surely therefore the contrasted formulae like 'sees and has seen' should mean simply that these pairs are compatible and *can* be true at the same time. This is the way the matter is explicitly put in *De Sophisticis Elenchis*, where Aristotle seeks to show that seeing belongs to a different category from making. He says (178a 9): 'Is it possible at the same time to make and to have made the same thing? No. But it is possible to see something and at the same time to have seen the same thing.' This way of understanding the 'sees and has seen' formulae yields, as has been said, a perfectly clear and relevant point about continuability.

There is, however, other evidence to support the view that Aristotle holds that the present entails the perfect in the case of energeia-verbs, even if this is not pointed out in the 'sees and has seen' passage of the *Metaphysics*. Firstly, the idea is naturally suggested by the distinction between activities which have and activities which lack a limit, the distinction drawn in the preceding section of the *Metaphysics* chapter. A limit points both ways. If you have already built a house you cannot still be building it; but also, if you are still building it you cannot yet have built it. There is a limit which both cannot be passed and must be reached. So, correspondingly, an action which altogether lacks a limit should be one not only continuable indefinitely but also fully performable in any period of time however short. If it could be true to say that a man Xes while denying that he has Xed the activity Xing would not 'lack a limit'; the man would still be on his way to a limit, viz. the point at which it would be true to say that he has Xed. Thus the general characterisation of perfect action in the earlier passage of the *Metaphysics* does suggest the idea that for such an action, an energeia, the present tense entails the perfect.

Secondly, a sentence in the *De Sensu* (446b 2) has this implication. The relevant words are in an 'if'—clause, but evidently express Aristotle's opinion. 'Everything at the same time hears and has heard, and in general perceives and has perceived, and there is no coming-into-being of them, but they *are* without *coming to be*.' I return later to these last phrases. The immediate point is that the word 'everything'—'everything at the same time hears and has heard'—seems to make this into a statement that 'hears' *entails* 'has heard'. Aristotle is not saying merely that 'hears and has heard' *can* hold, but that it does so in every case. Since he cannot mean that whenever anyone has heard something he must be going on doing so, he must mean that whenever anyone hears or is hearing it must also be the case that he has heard.

Further evidence that Aristotle does think this can be derived from his discussion of pleasure at the beginning of *Nicomachean Ethics* X. 4. But I postpone consideration of this passage, and ask next what exactly we are to suppose Aristotle to mean if he holds that in the case of energeia-verbs the present tense entails the perfect. Professor Ryle's suggestion on this deserves consideration. It has already been criticised in print (by Mr. R. J. Hirst in *The Problem of Perception*, Allen & Unwin, 1959, p. 132), but I believe that it still has adherents. I quote from *Dilemmas*, p. 102.

> . . . Seeing and hearing are not processes. Aristotle points out, quite correctly, that I can say 'I have seen it' as soon as I can say 'I see it'. To generalise the point that I think he is making, there are many verbs part of the business of which is to declare a terminus. To find something puts 'Finis' to searching for it; to win a race brings the race to an end. Other verbs are verbs of starting. To launch a boat is to inaugurate its career on the water; to found a college is to get it to exist from then on. Now starting and stopping cannot themselves have starts or stops, or, *a fortiori*, middles either. Noon does not begin, go on and finish. . . . It cannot itself go on for a time, however short. It is not a process or a state.
>
> It will, I think, be apparent why, with certain reservations, verbs which in this way declare termini cannot be used and are in fact not used in the continuous present or past tenses. . . . I can be looking for or looking at something, but I cannot be seeing it. At any given moment either I have not yet seen it or I have now seen it. The verb 'to see' does not signify an experience, i.e. something that I go through, am engaged in. It does not signify a sub-stretch of my life-story.

Ryle thus construes Aristotle's thesis that 'sees' entails 'has seen' as making the point that 'see' is a got-it verb and does not stand for anything that can go on for any time.

One fatal objection to this interpretation of Aristotle is to be found in the sentence already quoted, where Aristotle supports the statement that at the same time one lives well and has lived well by saying 'otherwise it would have to stop at some time'. This surely shows that he has in mind not a distinction between activities that go on through time and activities or acts that do not, but a contrast between activities whose character sets a limit to their continuance and activities whose character sets no limit. It is, of course, true that activities which do 'have to stop at some time' can*not* be achievements of the got-it kind, since these, so far from having to stop at some time, cannot ever stop (or start). But no one wishing to distinguish activities that go on through time from those that do not would do it by saying that the former 'have to stop at some time', since this so evidently suggests a contrast with those that *need* not stop, and not with those that cannot stop (or indeed start).

Secondly, whatever may be—or may have been thought by Aristotle to be—the case with 'see', some at least of the verbs that stand for energeiai as opposed to kineseis in Aristotle are certainly not got-it verbs. Thinking (νοεῖν) or contemplating (θεωρεῖν, *Metaphysics* Θ. 8. 1050a 36) is certainly an activity one can be engaged in for a time. Thus in *Metaphysics* Λ. 7. 1072b 14–30 God is contrasted with men because he thinks continuously and eternally, while they can do so only for a short period of time (μικρὸν χρόνον). In *Nicomachean Ethics* X. 7. 1177a 21 the activity of thought or contemplation is said to be the most continuous (and, in particular, more continuous than practical activity): 'since we can contemplate more continuously than we can *do* anything'. Again, the continuability through time of living or living well, and of being happy, other examples of energeiai, is obvious. Since Aristotle uses one and the same linguistic test to segregate seeing from kineseis and to segregate thinking, living well, etc., from kineseis, it cannot be right to construe his point about 'see' in a way that makes nonsense when applied to his other examples.

Thirdly, there is the general consideration that the Greek verbs translated 'see' and 'hear' correspond, in fact, not only to 'see' and 'hear' but also to 'look at' or 'keep in view' and 'listen to'; and further, that they have perfectly good continuous past tenses (they cannot be blamed for not having a present continuous form, since there is no such form in Greek). Clearly, then, the odds were very much against Aristotle's seeing, let alone clearly expressing, Ryle's point about perception-verbs.

I conclude that it is no part of Aristotle's view of energeiai that they cannot go on through time, and that his energeiai-verbs do not correspond to Ryle's got-it verbs. (They have a better chance of corresponding to Ryle's other class of achievement verbs, the 'keeping' ones.)

If 'everything at the same time hears and has heard' does not make Ryle's point, an obvious alternative is to hand. The 'has heard' can be taken to refer to a period of time preceding the moment to which the 'hears' refers.

First, let us say something that holds of both kineseis and energeiai. If a man *starts* to X at time *t* he cannot be said to *be* Xing at *t*; it is only at some moment later than *t*, say *w*, that he can be said to be Xing. Since no two moments are contiguous there must be an interval between *t* and *w*; and however short this period (*t* to *w*), it is a period of Xing preceding the moment *w* at which the man is said to be Xing. Thus, as soon as it is true to say 'he is Xing' it is true to say 'he has been Xing'. Aristotle argues for all this at some length in *Physics* VI. 5 and 6, claiming that there is no absolutely first sub-period in a period of change or movement, but that 'everything that is in motion must have been in motion before' (236b 33).

Let us now take an example—an example of a kinesis as opposed to an energeia. If at *w* a man is building a house he must have started to build at some time *t* prior to *w*, and he must have been at it for some period before *w*. However, it clearly does *not* follow from the fact that we can say at *w* 'he is building a house' that we cay say at *w*—with reference to the preceding period—'he has built a house'. Indeed, this we certainly can*not* say. With energeiai, however, the case is different; with energeiai 'he is Xing' *entails* 'he has Xed'. The perfect can always be used of the period preceding a moment at which the present can be used.

If at *w* a man is playing a prelude he must have been at it for some time; but what he has done in that time cannot be described by saying 'he has played a prelude'; nor, had he fallen dead at *w*, could we have included as the last item in his biography the statement 'he played a prelude'. But if at *w* he is gazing at a statue, not only must he have been doing so for some time, but what he has done in that time entitles us to say at *w* 'he has gazed at the statue'; and had he fallen dead at *w* his biography could have included at the end the statement 'he gazed at the statue'. So playing a prelude qualifies as a kinesis, gazing at a statue as an energeia.

While Ryle's account of the present–perfect connection involves that an energeia cannot go on through time, this one implies that it must. There may be objections to thinking that seeing, for example, must occupy time, and even objections to thinking that Aristotle thought this. But the passages so far considered do not provide any evidence against the belief that Aristotle did think this. The *Metaphysics* passage, in particular, does not suggest the idea that an energeia cannot (or need not) occupy time; but rather that there is no upper or lower limit to the time it may occupy, and that it is somehow equally and fully present throughout any such period.

III. NICOMACHEAN ETHICS X. 4

Aristotle does not say that he is here talking of the distinction between energeiai and kineseis. But he likens pleasure or enjoyment (ἡδονή) to seeing, and contrasts both with kineseis, using as examples of kineseis house-building and walking—which were also used as examples of kineseis in the *Metaphysics* passage. Both the choice of examples and the general account of the contrast leave no doubt that it *is* the energeia–kinesis distinction that he is using. Moreover, though he is going to say that enjoyment somehow *perfects* energeia (rather than that it *is* an energeia) it is fair to say, for the purposes of the present discussion and on the basis of X. 4. 1–4, that he classifies enjoying on the energeia side of the energeia–kinesis distinction.

> Seeing seems to be, with respect to any time whatever, perfect. For it does not lack anything whose coming into being later will perfect its form (τελειώσει αὐτῆς τὸ εἶδος); and pleasure also seems to be of this nature. For it is a whole, and at no time can one find a pleasure whose form will be completed if the pleasure lasts longer. For this reason too it is not a kinesis. For every kinesis (e.g. that of building) is in a time and for the sake of an end, and is perfect when it has made what it aims at. It is perfect therefore only in the whole time or at that final moment. In their parts and during the time they occupy, all kineseis are imperfect, and are different in kind from the whole kinesis and from each other (1174a 14–23).

Aristotle then proceeds to mention some of the different phases in the kinesis of building a temple (1174a 23–9).

The distinction between the form which is and the form which is not perfect with respect to any time whatever can most naturally be elucidated in terms of what can be said at various times. With a kinesis the form is not perfect with respect to any time whatever: the perfect tense is applicable only at the end of a stretch of time at the end of none of whose sub-stretches it was applicable. With an energeia the form is perfect with respect to any time whatever: the perfect tense is applicable at any moment in a stretch of time occupied by that energeia, that is, at the end of any sub-

128

stretch however short. 'Is gazing at the statue' entails 'has gazed at the statue'; 'is building the house' is inconsistent with 'has built the house'. If this is the correct interpretation of the *Ethics* distinction it confirms that Aristotle does hold that with energeia-verbs the present entails the perfect, and it confirms the way in which this was understood above (in opposition to Ryle's account).

It may be objected that Aristotle cannot mean to characterise energeiai in such a way that an energeia must go on through time, since he says (1174a 19) 'every kinesis is in a time and for the sake of an end'. If in distinguishing energeiai from kineseis he says that every kinesis is 'in a time' is he not implying that an energeia need not occupy time? It is wrong, however, to regard the words 'in a time and for the sake of an end' as giving two independent criteria for being a kinesis. There is no further suggestion in the context that occupying time (or necessarily occupying time) by itself distinguishes kineseis from energeiai. The words 'in a time and for the sake of an end' go closely together to give a single criterion; a kinesis occupies some *definite* time limited by its arrival at its end, that is, its goal. The phrase makes the same point as is made in the *Metaphysics* by the equating of having a limit with having an end; there also the contrast was not with something occupying no time but with something which did not occupy a fixed time determined by the goal to be reached. That Aristotle is in the *Ethics* making this *single* point when he says 'every kinesis is in a time and for the sake of an end' is confirmed by the way he goes on: 'and it is perfect when it has made what it aims at. It is perfect, therefore, only in the whole time or at that final moment.' Here, in what is evidently intended to explain the preceding short statement, the notions of end or goal and time are blended to provide a single criterion for being a kinesis, viz. that only at the termination of a fixed period of time, or perhaps with reference to the whole of such a period, can a kinesis be called perfect—the period, of course, being fixed by the necessity of reaching the appropriate goal. Thus the *Ethics* discussion, down to 1174b 7, contains no suggestion that an energeia can occur without going on for any time.

After the discussion so far summarised has come (at 1174b 7) to its conclusion that enjoyment is not a kinesis but is something 'whole and perfect', Aristotle adds a further and different reason for the conclusion. He says: 'This would seem to be the case, too, from the fact that it is not possible to undergo kinesis otherwise than in a time, but it is possible to have enjoyment [or perhaps, 'be pleased']; for what occurs in the 'now' is something complete (τὸ γὰρ ἐν τῷ νῦν ὅλον τι).' That this is added as a *supplementary* argument confirms that in the preceding discussion Aristotle was not making the point that energeiai can occur in the 'now' while kineseis cannot. However, it might be thought that this later statement that it is possible to have enjoyment in the 'now'— 'otherwise than in a time'—is inconsistent with the distinction drawn in the preceding passage, if it was there assumed that energeiai go on through time. I am not quite clear what to say about this, for I am not sure what fact Aristotle is pointing to when he says that enjoyment or pleasure may occur 'not in a time'. But certainly the rule or criterion here suggested (rule 1), 'if Xing can occur not in a time it is not a kinesis' does not seem *inconsistent* with the rule implied in the previous discussion (rule 2), 'if at every moment in a period of Xing it is true to say "he has Xed", then Xing is not a kinesis'. Now if, as I have argued, Aristotle believes that any energeia can go on through time, while it is evident that not every energeia can occur *not* in a time (e.g. living or living well), it is not surprising that Aristotle should have given his main accounts of the distinction between energeiai and kineseis by reference to cases where energeiai do go on through time, that is, by using rule 2.

Indeed, granted that any energeia may continue through time, the first rule—'if Xing can occur not in a time it is not a kinesis' —does not provide an adequate way of distinguishing energeiai from kineseis. That Xing can occur not in a time shows, by rule 1, that it is not a kinesis (the point Aristotle is insisting on with regard to enjoyment), but it does not show that it is an energeia. For the starts and terminations of kineseis are not in a time—do not last for any time—yet they are not themselves energeiai. So rule 1 can establish that Xing is not a kinesis, but only rule 2 can establish that Xing is an energeia. In short, if Aristotle recognised the possibility of using some energeia-verbs to stand for duration-less acts, he threw this in as an additional contrast to kineseis-verbs, but he did not make this possibility either a necessary or a sufficient condition for being an energeia-verb. The necessary and sufficient condition for being an energeia-verb is that rule 2 be satisfied. Aristotle's main accounts of the distinction between energeiai and kineseis do not presuppose that if Xing is an energeia Xing must always occupy time. They do assume that if Xing is an energeia Xing may go on through time, and they give a criterion for distinguishing energeiai from kineseis by reference to the behaviour of energeia-verbs in situations where they are used to describe what is going on through time.

IV. A DIFFICULTY

I turn now to the main and obvious difficulty about Aristotle's account of energeia and kinesis. In both the *Metaphysics* and the *Ethics* passages he gives walking (βαδίζειν) as an example of a kinesis. But how can this be so, if the criterion for X's being a kinesis is that 'he has Xed' cannot be true of any part of a period of the whole of which it is true? For are not parts of walks walks? Now Aristotle perhaps realises that what he has said about kineseis as opposed to energeiai does not fit walking so easily as house-building. At any rate he follows his discussion of building in the *Ethics* with a separate section on walking (1174a 29–b 5). He argues that in walking (as in other forms of locomotion like flying) 'the whence and whither constitute the form' (τὸ πόθεν ποῖ εἰδοποιόν). In other words, he claims that no part of a walk does qualify for the same specific description as any other part of the walk or as the whole walk. If I walk from Oxford to Reading the 'form' of the whole walk is its being a walk from Oxford to Reading, and this form is not achieved until I have reached Reading. Then, but at no earlier stage, can I say 'I have walked from Oxford to Reading'. I could earlier, on arrival at Wallingford, have said 'I have walked from Oxford to Wallingford'—but that again I could not have said at any time preceding the time of arrival at Wallingford.

Now certainly we can, as Aristotle tells us, provide different descriptions for the parts and the whole of any walk. Nor are the differences in question trivial or irrelevant: it is not as if Aristotle had distinguished portions of a walk by temporal references, which one could clearly do equally well for sub-stretches of a period of an energeia. Yet, granted that such different descriptions of parts of a walk and of the whole walk are always possible, and germane to what has been done *qua* walking, why cannot the same procedure be used to show that, say, enjoyment can be a kinesis? Enjoyment, as Aristotle himself insists, is always the enjoyment of something; and that something may be a play, a symphony, or a battle. Suppose I have enjoyed hearing a symphony; this description—'I have enjoyed hearing the symphony' is the full and proper description of what I have done, just as, if I have walked from A to Z, the proper description of what I have done is, according to Aristotle, 'I have walked from A to Z'. But 'I have enjoyed the symphony' is *not* something I can say 'with respect to any time whatever'—at the end of any sub-stretch of the total period—any more than 'I have walked from A to Z' is. If called away in the middle of the symphony I could not say that I had enjoyed hearing the symphony or that I had heard the symphony (any more than the players if interrupted could say that they had played the symphony). In short, the procedure by which Aristotle makes walking count as a kinesis and not an energeia—the procedure of taking relatively precise or specific descriptions of walks and showing that *they* do not apply to parts of the walks—can be applied also to enjoying, hearing, etc. If the rules for saying 'he has walked from A to Z' prove that walking is a kinesis, don't the rules for saying 'he has heard the symphony' or 'he has enjoyed hearing the symphony' prove that hearing and enjoying are kineseis too?

It is not open to Aristotle to argue that hearing is after all an energeia because in every part of the time during which the man was listening to the symphony he could be said to have heard, or to have heard something. For his proof that walking is a kinesis depends upon asking, not whether the man who walked from A to Z could be said to have walked, or to have walked somewhere, in sub-stretches of the time he took to go from A to Z, but whether he could be said to have walked from A to Z in such sub-stretches. Thus Aristotle could not claim that though hearing a symphony is a kinesis hearing is an energeia without having to admit that though walking from A to Z is a kinesis walking is an energeia.

The difficulty would, of course, be removed if it could be shown that Aristotle did not intend 'enjoy', 'hear', 'think', etc., to cover the kind of case that the objection brings forward, but that he had in mind only such cases as enjoying a scent, hearing a single sound, dwelling on a single truth. But such a restriction on the meaning of the terms would be utterly alien to ordinary Greek usage and not supported by Aristotle's usage elsewhere. Indeed, the point about enjoyment in the *Ethics* is embedded in a discussion which assumes—of course—that one can enjoy all sorts of complex activities and experiences. Again, while the verbs translated 'think' and 'contemplate' are sometimes used by Aristotle of the grasp or contemplation of single truths, they are equally used for trains of thought or ratiocination. So had Aristotle been clear that he wanted to classify as energeiai only certain cases of hearing, enjoying, thinking, etc., he could not possibly have spoken as he does, using the verbs without qualification.

It might be suggested that Aristotle is entitled to classify walking as a kinesis because variant descriptions can always be found for the parts and the whole, and that he is entitled to classify hearing, etc., as energeiai because variant descriptions cannot always be found. Walking is always from some *A* to some *Z*, while hearing can be the hearing of a continuous unchanging note. But this defence of Aristotle fails. Firstly, he does not say or suggest that seeing and enjoying are energeiai because *some* instances of them satisfy the requirement 'perfect with respect to any time whatsoever'; he says without restriction that *they* satisfy this requirement. Secondly, if the key to the distinction between energeiai and kineseis is the notion of 'perfection with respect to any time whatsoever', and if some cases of enjoyment, etc., satisfy this and others do not, the only and obvious conclusion is that some enjoyment, etc., is energeia and some is kinesis.

It is appropriate at this point to refer to a comment Ryle has made about Aristotle's treatment of pleasure. The view that he attributes to Aristotle (evidently on the basis of our passage) might make our difficulty about enjoying a symphony—and how you cannot be said to have done so until the end of it—irrelevant to Aristotle's thesis. I quote from Ryle's paper 'Proofs in Philosophy' (*Revue Internationale de Philosophie*, 1954).

> If enjoying something were a process from state to state, it would follow that a person could have begun to enjoy something but been prevented from finishing, as a person can begin his dinner but be prevented from completing it. But though a person may enjoy something for a short time or for a long time, he cannot have half an enjoyment. Enjoyments can be great or small, but not fractional.

It is rather remarkable that Ryle can, as we saw, interpret Aristotle's remarks about seeing and other energeiai in the *Metaphysics* as meaning that they are not processes and cannot go on for a time, and can now interpret the *Ethics* passage, in which enjoyment is likened to seeing and contrasted with kineseis, as meaning that enjoyment is not a process but can last for a time. It is hard to see how both these interpretations of the energeia–kinesis distinction could be right. In fact, the second as well as the first seems to be wrong. It would, indeed, be odd to speak of having half an enjoyment, and fairly odd to speak of being prevented from finishing enjoying something. But these are not translations of any phrases Aristotle uses. *He* does not, to make *his* point, exploit any such words as 'interrupt', 'prevent from finishing', 'complete', or 'half'. His distinction depends on whether an activity is or is not 'perfect with respect to any time whatsoever', and this surely is a question whether one can or cannot apply the same description—ascribe the same 'form'—to every sub-stretch of a given stretch. So what Ryle says is clearly not a direct interpretation of Aristotle's words. But it is not even a correct expansion of them. For Ryle's class of expressions X such that one cannot speak of being prevented from finishing Xing is not the same as Aristotle's class of expressions Y such that one can say 'he has Yed' at any moment in a period of Ying. Consider 'enjoying the Choral Symphony'. This will go into Ryle's class of X-expressions, but not into Aristotle's class of Y-expressions. In general, that it is absurd to speak of being 'prevented from finishing' Xing does not entail that one can say 'he has Xed' at any moment in a period of Xing.

Thus Ryle's interesting remarks about enjoying are not an acceptable exegesis of Aristotle, and do nothing to remove the major difficulty that has been raised. This difficulty, to repeat, is that while Aristotle's *descriptions* of his energeia–kinesis distinction seem to add up to a useful distinction, his treatment of examples is not in accordance with that distinction. Nor can this be shrugged off by saying that anyone is liable to throw in an infelicitous example. For 'enjoying' is no casual example, but the very topic of the *Ethics* passage; while Aristotle goes out of his way to discuss walking at some length and to explain why it is to count as a kinesis. Yet it was precisely the cases of walking and enjoying that were used above to show up the major difficulty.

We seem, therefore, forced to conclude that there is a serious confusion in Aristotle's exposition of the energeia–kinesis distinction.

V. RECAPITULATION

I can perhaps pull together what has been said by quoting a passage from Professor Zeno Vendler's excellent paper 'Times and Tenses' (*Philosophical Review*, 1957). Vendler's distinction between what he calls activities and accomplishments seems to be the distinction Aristotle is telling us to make in his accounts of the energeia–kinesis distinction, while the examples Vendler uses to illustrate the distinction bring out clearly how unjustified Aristotle is in his blanket classification of hearing, etc., as energeiai and walking, etc., as kineseis. I have interposed a few references to Aristotle; Vendler himself does not refer to him.

First let us focus our attention on the group of verbs that admit continuous tenses. There is a marked cleavage within the group itself. If I say that someone is running or pushing a cart, my statement does not imply any assumption as to how long that running or pushing will go on; he might stop the next moment or he might keep running or pushing for half an hour ['lacks a limit']. On the other hand, if I say of a person that he is running a mile or of someone else that he is drawing a circle, then I do claim that the first one will keep running till he has covered the mile and that the second will keep drawing till he has drawn the circle. If they do not complete their activities, my statement will turn out to be false. Thus we see that while running or pushing a cart have no set terminal point ['lacks a limit'], running a mile and drawing a circle do have a "climax", which has to be reached if the action is to be what it is claimed to be. In other words, if someone stops running a mile, he did not run a mile; if one stops drawing a circle, he did not draw a circle. But the man who stops running did run, and he who stops pushing the cart did push it. Running a mile and drawing a circle have to be finished, while it does not make sense to talk of finishing running or pushing a cart. . . . If it is true that someone has been running for half an hour, then it must be true that he has been running for every period within that half-hour ['perfect with respect to any time whatever', 'lacking nothing whose coming into being later will perfect its form']. But even if it is true that a runner has run a mile in four minutes, it cannot be true that he has run a mile in any period which is a real part of that time, although it remains true that he was running, or that he was engaged in running a mile during any

135

substretch of those four minutes. Similarly, in case I wrote a letter in an hour, I did not write it in, say, the first quarter of the hour. It appears, then, that running and its kind go on in time in a homogeneous way ['form perfect with respect to any time whatever']; any part of the process is of the same nature as the whole. Not so with running a mile or writing a letter. . . . Let us call the first type, that of "running", "pushing a cart", and so forth *activity terms*, and the second type, that of "running a mile", "drawing a circle", and so forth *accomplishment terms*.

VI. OTHER TEXTS

The last section of this paper will contain a brief discussion of some further passages which might be expected to throw light on the energeia–kinesis distinction.

(*a*) In *Nicomachean Ethics* X. 3 Aristotle says that pleasure is not a kinesis: 'for speed and slowness seem to be proper to every kinesis . . . but neither of these holds of pleasure. For while we may *become* pleased quickly (as we may *become* angry quickly) we cannot *be* pleased quickly . . . while we *can* walk or grow or the like quickly.' Now one certainly might divide verbs into two classes according to whether they do or do not admit qualification by the adverbs 'quickly' and slowly'. But the suggestion that here we have the real ground for Aristotle's distinction between energeiai and kineseis is not convincing. First, Aristotle does not exploit this elsewhere as a criterion for distinguishing energeiai from kineseis. Next, he does not, even here, state in a general way that all energeiai-verbs refuse, while all kinesis-verbs accept, such adverbial qualifications. Finally, though this adverbial criterion may indicate a philosophically important distinction between two types of verbs, one would expect it to be backed up and in a way explained by a fairly general characterisation of the types of activity concerned. Since Aristotle attempts such a general account, particularly in the *Metaphysics* and *Ethics* passages examined earlier, it seems proper to examine *these* to see what the distinction amounts to, rather than to rely upon one brief and ungeneralised reference to the adverbial criterion.

(*b*) In the *De Sensu* passage already quoted (446b 2), after saying that 'everything at the same time hears and has heard, and in general perceives and has perceived', Aristotle goes on: 'and there is no coming into being of them, but they *are* without *coming to be*'. Is this a new clue to the energeia–kinesis distinction? In the *Ethics*, too (X. 4. 1174b 12–13), after the proof that pleasure, like seeing, is not a coming into being or a kinesis, Aristotle remarks that there is no coming into being *of* seeing or *of* pleasure. Unfortunately, it is hard to understand why Aristotle thinks it worth pointing this out in connection with the distinction between energeiai and kineseis, for he holds that there is no coming into being of a kinesis either. The point is stated and argued in *Physics* V. 2. 'There is not any kinesis of a kinesis, nor coming into being of a coming into being, nor in general change of change' (225b 15). The obvious candidates for things *of* which there is a coming into being—things which can*not* 'be without coming to be'—would be products of processes of making or terminal states following processes of change. But such products or states are relevant to the distinction between energeiai and kineseis only in so far as kineseis are processes *leading to* such products or states, that is, are (in a broad sense) comings-into-being, while energeiai are not. But this is simply to repeat the point Aristotle has already made, that energeiai are not themselves comings-into-being or kineseis. It seems impossible to construe the statement that there is no coming into being *of* seeing in such a way as to make it relevant to the distinction between energeiai and kineseis, *without* construing it (or misconstruing it) as *equivalent* to the statement that seeing is not itself a coming into being. But then it does not offer any additional clue to the nature of the distinction under examination.

(*c*) It may be thought that I have wrongly neglected an important element in Aristotle's thinking about energeiai and kineseis, the idea that energeiai are desired or desirable for their own sakes while kineseis are not. Two different suggestions are possible: (1) that Aristotle actually draws the distinction between energeiai and kineseis with the aid of a psychological or evaluative criterion, that is, in terms of human desires as they are or as they ought to be; (2) that Aristotle does indeed draw the distinction in quite other terms (as has been supposed above), but that he is improperly influenced in his classifying of various candidates into the two classes by psychological or evaluative considerations. This latter would be a suggestion to explain discrepancies between Aristotle's account of his distinction and his treatment of particular examples; it would presuppose that there is some confusion in

J. L. ACKRILL

what he says. Since this paper is concerned only to show up the confusion this suggested diagnosis of its cause can be left aside.

The first suggestion would presumably rely on the fact that in the *Metaphysics* and *Ethics* passages Aristotle uses such expressions as 'end' or 'goal', 'aims at', 'for the sake of' (τέλος, ἐφίεται, οὗ ἕνεκα). But Aristotle constantly uses such terms in contexts where no question of human or other conscious purpose or motive arises; and in the absence of any more definite indication that Aristotle is distinguishing energeiai from kineseis by a test which has to do with desires and motives it would be very rash to assume this. That house-building is directed to the production of a house, has a house as its aim or goal, is, surely, not put forward as a fact about the motivation of builders, but as a fact about the concept of house-building (a fact that can be expressed by the formula 'it is not true that at the same time one builds a house and has built it'). There may be logical, psychological, or ethical connections between the question whether Xing is an energeia or a kinesis and the question whether people can, do, or ought to X for its own sake. But Aristotle does not seem to advocate answering the latter question as the way to discover the answer to the former question.

(*d*) In *Physics* III Aristotle asks what kinesis is. He says that 'kinesis seems to be a kind of energeia, but imperfect' (201b 30), and he goes on: 'the reason is that the potentiality whose energeia it is, is imperfect'. Now, since energeia in the narrow sense is itself in general the actualisation of a potentiality, the suggestion here is that kinesis is an imperfect actualisation because it is the actualisation of a certain type of potentiality, an imperfect one. One might, therefore, ask what makes a *potentiality* imperfect or not, in the hope of distinguishing kinesis from energeia (in the narrow sense) indirectly, *via* the distinction between the types of potentiality of which each is the actualisation. This is, of course, not the sort of procedure we expect to find Aristotle adopting or permitting, since he regularly insists that actuality is prior to potentiality in definition (λόγῳ) as well as in other ways, and we should therefore expect to find different types of potentiality defined in terms of differences between the respective actualisations, and not vice versa. If we hopefully neglect this point, and try to elucidate further the remarks in the *Physics*, we shall naturally turn to Aristotle's more or less formal definition of kinesis in *Physics* III.

138

1. 201a 11: 'the entelechy of that which is potentially, as such' (ἡ τοῦ δυνάμει ὄντος ἐντελέχεια, ᾗ τοιοῦτον); or 201b 5: 'the entelechy of the potential, *qua* potential' (ἡ τοῦ δυνατοῦ, ᾗ δυνατόν, ἐντελέχεια). Though the word 'energeia' is not used in these phrases, it and its verb occur often throughout the discussion; and it will not be misleading for present purposes to equate 'entelechy' with 'energeia' (in the broad sense of 'actualisation').

Now at first sight these definitions suggest that a kinesis is not the actualisation of a certain *kind* of potentiality (an imperfect one), but the actualisation of potentiality in a certain aspect or way—'as such', '*qua* potential'. If, however, one asks what this kind of way is, one finds that only *some* potentialities are capable of being actualised in this way, and that *they* are not capable of being actualised in any other way. The potentiality capable of being actualised 'as such', '*qua* potentiality', is in fact just the *imperfect* potentiality. I quote Ross's note on *Physics* III. 1. 201a 9–b 15, where Aristotle explains his definition of kinesis with the aid of the example of house-building: the process of building is the actualisation of the buildable *qua* buildable.

> An aggregate of bricks, stones etc., may be regarded (1) as so many bricks, stones etc., (2) as potentially a house, (3) as potentially being in course of being fashioned into a house. The kinesis of building is the actualisation not (1) of the materials *as* these materials (they are, previously to the kinesis of building, already actually those materials), nor (2) of their potentiality of being a house (the *house* is the actualisation of this), but (3) of their potentiality of being fashioned into a house. Similarly every kinesis is an actualisation-of-a-potentiality which is a stage on the way to a further actualisation of potentiality, and only exists while the further potentiality is not yet actualised. Hence it is imperfect, and, though in a sense an energeia, is distinct from an energeia in the narrower sense in which 'energeia' implies that no element of potentiality is present at all.

[I have written 'kinesis' where Ross writes 'movement', and 'actualisation' where he writes 'realisation'; I have transliterated one or two words he writes in Greek.]

Thus the question whether a potentiality is imperfect *is* the question whether it is of the sort that is actualised '*qua* potential', i.e. over a period of time during no part of which it is fully actualised (for there remains an element of potentiality) and at the end of which it ceases to be being actualised (for there is no longer any potentiality). So the different-looking phrases in the *Physics* take us back in fact to the test indicated in the *Metaphysics* and *Ethics*: one can establish that Xing is an energeia and not a kinesis if one can establish that it is not the actualisation of an *imperfect* potentiality or of a potentiality '*qua* potential'; but one can establish this only by establishing that what is being done in any period of actual Xing is the same as what is being done in any other such period, that is, that the 'form' is perfect 'with respect to any time whatever'. The *Physics* account of kinesis does not, therefore, provide any new independent criterion for the distinction between kinesis and energeia.

(*e*) If the *Physics* account of kinesis as the actualisation of what is imperfect simply leads us back to the criterion of the *Metaphysics* and *Ethics*, the same phrase serves to make a rather different point in the *De Anima*. At III. 7. 431a 4–7 Aristotle says that the transition from potential to actual perceiving is not a case of alteration or indeed of kinesis at all: 'for kinesis, as we said, is an actualisation of the *imperfect*; actualisation in the unqualified sense —that is, of what is perfect—is different'. The word translated 'as we said' is omitted by most manuscripts. But in any case the reader will naturally refer back to II. 5, where again the distinction between potential and actual seeing and thinking is under discussion, and where kinesis is said to be 'a kind of actualisation, but imperfect'. In this chapter two types of potentiality are distinguished. Since an example of the actualisation of one type is learning, and examples of actualisations of the other type are perceiving and thinking, we might hope to find in this distinction of types of potentiality an elucidation of the energeia–kinesis distinction, for which perceiving and thinking, and on the other hand learning, are standard examples. In fact, however, Aristotle's explanation of the two types of potentiality in *De Anima* II. 5 reveals quite a different distinction. He contrasts, roughly, first-order abilities, abilities to do things, with second-order abilities, abilities to acquire first-order abilities. He says that in exercising a second-order ability one is undergoing a change, developing one's nature (φύσις); while in exercising a first-order ability one is not undergoing a change, one is simply exercising or expressing one's nature. A man capable of acquiring certain knowledge is in that respect imperfect—his nature remains not fully developed; the process of *acquiring* it is a journey towards an end or goal arrival at which will make him (as far as this field of knowledge goes) perfect or perfected. He then *has* certain knowledge, that is, he has the ability to use it. When he does *this* he is exploiting or expressing his perfected nature, not changing it or moving towards a further end or goal.

Aristotle, then, distinguishes between getting, having, and using a (first-order) ability; and he says that getting such an ability is undergoing a kinesis, but using it is not a kinesis but an energeia. It is clear that this distinction, in spite of similarity of terminology and examples, is utterly different from that drawn elsewhere between energeia and kinesis. For the distinction between acquiring and using an ability can itself be applied as well to (say) house-building as to (say) knowledge of mathematics. When a *skilled* man builds a house this will not, according to the *De Anima* distinction, be a kinesis but an energeia; for the man is not changing but expressing his nature, not acquiring but exercising a perfection. Aristotle himself recognises this; he says that 'it is not right to say that a wise man is altered whenever he displays wisdom, any more than that a house-builder is when he builds a house' (417b 8–9). Thus the *De Anima* distinction, though valuable in itself, is not the same as the usual energeia–kinesis distinction. It tells us when to say that a man engaged in an activity is thereby *undergoing* a kinesis, but it does not tell us which of the activities a man may be engaged in are themselves kineseis. If Callias, a skilled man, is building a house, we are not to say that he is being changed (undergoing a kinesis); yet what he is doing, house-building, is, of course, a paradigm case of an activity that is a kinesis and not an energeia. Some connection might be found between the distinction between acquiring and using abilities and the usual distinction between kinesis and energeia; but the connection is not obvious and is certainly not asserted or explained by Aristotle.

THOUGHT AND ACTION
IN ARISTOTLE
WHAT IS 'PRACTICAL TRUTH'?
G. E. M. Anscombe

IS Aristotle inconsistent in the different things he says about προαιρεσις, mostly translated "choice", in the different parts of the *Ethics*? The following seems to be a striking inconsistency. In Book III (113a 4) he says that what is "decided by deliberation" is chosen (το ἐκ της βουλης κριθεν προαιρετον ἐστιν), but he also often insists that the uncontrolled man, the ἀκρατης, does not *choose* to do what he does; that is to say, what he does in doing the kind of thing that he disapproves of, is not what Aristotle will call exercising choice; the uncontrolled man does not act from choice, ἐκ προαιρεσεως, or choosing, προαιρουμενος. However, in Book VI (1142b 18) he mentions the possibility of a calculating uncontrolled man who will get what he arrived at by calculation, ἐκ του λογισμου τευξεται, and so will have deliberated correctly: ὀρθως ἐσται βεβουλευμενος. Thus we have the three theses: (*a*) choice is what is determined by deliberation; (*b*) what the uncontrolled man does *qua* uncontrolled, he does not choose to do; (*c*) the uncontrolled man, even when acting against his convictions, does on occasion determine what to do by deliberation.

Without a doubt the set of passages is inconsistent if we are to understand that any case of something being determined by deliberation at all is a case of choice, as seems to be suggested by the formulation "what is decided by deliberation is chosen".

If, then, Aristotle is consistent, perhaps his 'choice' is not *simply* determination by calculating or deliberating. There is some reason to think this; though he says that what is determined by deliberation (κριθεν ἐκ τῆς βουλῆς) *is* chosen, we may say that the *context* shows that he himself has in mind a deliberation what to do with a view to one's ends, and that ends are things like being honoured, health, the life of virtue, or material prosperity, or enjoyment of knowledge, or sensual pleasure. The uncontrolled man, the ἀκρατης, is not one whose general object is, say, enjoying a life of sensual pleasure; he simply has the *particular* purpose of seducing his neighbour's wife.

On this view, we remove the inconsistency by saying that 'choice' is of something determined not just by any deliberation, but by deliberation how to obtain an object of one's *will* (βουλησις) rather than merely of one's *desire* (ἐπιθυμια): there will be a contrast here even for the ἀκολαστος, the licentious man. For *his* will is *to satisfy his desires, his sensual appetites*; and his decision to seduce his neighbour's wife, say, is a 'choice', as well as being an expression of his lusts, just because his end in life *is* to satisfy his lusts; this has to be shown before one can say that a man who is going after objects of 'desire' evilly, has a bad 'choice'.

Now—though I think this does represent Aristotle's view—an objection that strikes one is that people's 'ends' aren't in general nearly as definitely one thing or another as Aristotle makes out. *If* 'will' (βουλησις) is simply the type of wanting (ὀρεξις) that one has in relation to one's final objective *in* what one is deliberately doing at any time, then there seems no objection to saying that the weak man at 1151a 2 (the uncontrolled man who calculates how to get what tempts him, for he is surely a man of the weak rather than the impulsive type) has a *will* to seduce his neighbour's wife, or a will for the pleasure of it, at the time when he is cleverly reckoning how to do it. The fact that he has a bad conscience about it doesn't seem to be either here or there *for determining whether he is making that his aim* for the time being; but this fact, that he has a bad conscience about it, *is* just what makes him uncontrolled rather than licentious, ἀκρατης rather than ἀκολαστος.

There is, however, another defence against the charge of inconsistency, which perhaps is not open to the objection that it requires an unrealistic idea of the clearcutness of people's ends. Not all deliberation is with a view to making a 'choice', forming a προαιρεσις, where none has yet been made; some deliberation is with a view to executing a 'choice'. This is made clear at 1144a 20;

"Virtue makes one's choice right, but as for what has to be done for the sake of it, that doesn't belong to virtue but to another power—cleverness." τὴν μὲν οὖν προαιρεσιν ὀρθὴν ποιει ἡ ἀρετη. το δ'ὅσα ἐκεινης ἑνεκα πεφυκε πραττεσθαι οὐκ ἐστι της ἀρετης ἀλλ' ἑτερας δυναμεως.

But also in Book III Aristotle speaks of *trying* to do the thing that a deliberation has terminated in: "if it seems possible, they try to do it. Possible things are the things that *might* come about through us" (1112b 26). So we might say that something that seems to be a way of achieving your end and to be possible may be decided upon; *that* you will do this (or at least will try) is a 'choice'; and now there may be further deliberation just how to manage that possible-seeming thing. Now in Book III there is no suggestion that wanting (ὄρεξις of) the more immediate means (adopted to execute the remoter means that have already been decided on) is not itself *also* a 'choice', προαιρεσις. But if we are to reconcile the denial (which *also* occurs in Book III 1111b 14) that the uncontrolled man acts *choosing* so to act (προαιρουμενος) with the account in Book VI of a calculating uncontrolled man, then we must say that when deliberation how to execute a decision terminates in an action—the man contrives a skilful approach to the woman—this will not be a case of 'choice' if the decision was not reached by deliberation.

Thus the passages in which Aristotle describes deliberation as going on till we have reached something we can do here and now, and describes 'choice' as being of what deliberation has reached, must not lead us to think that matter for a 'choice' has *only* been reached when there is no more room for deliberation of any kind.

On the other hand, just as the first defence left us wondering what Aristotle supposed a βουλησις, a case of 'will', to be, since apparently the pleasure sought by the uncontrolled man who calculates is not an object of his will; so this defence leaves us in the dark as to what a 'choice' is. We may well have thought we knew this; for 'what you can do here and now, which you have reached as a result of deliberating how to achieve an end'—the first cause (πρωτον αἰτιον), the last thing in analysis and first in execution—did seem a relatively clear notion. But if, as must be admitted on the basis of the text, there is room for calculating how to execute a 'choice', then just where in the chain of deliberations from an end to the immediate thing that I can do without having to consider *how* to do it—just where in this chain does the first 'choice' come?

It must be admitted that Aristotle's account of deliberation (βουλευσις, or βουλη) often seems to fit deliberation about how to execute a decision, and in particular to fit technical deliberation, better than deliberation which is about the means here and now to 'living well in general'—προς το ευ ζην ολως. It seems at its clearest when he is describing the doctor deliberating how to restore health by reducing the imbalance of humours by . . ., etc. But this is a piece of technical deliberation.

I am not saying that Aristotle so uses "προαιρεσις" ("choice") that the termination of a piece of technical deliberation isn't a 'choice'. On the contrary; that would, I think, be quite inconsistent with the treatment in Book III. But Book VI teaches us, as I think we might not have realised from Book III, that there is no such thing as a 'choice' which is *only* technical (I use "technical" to cover practical cleverness in bringing particular situations about, even when it's not strictly a technique that's in question). There is always, on Aristotle's view, another 'choice' behind a technical or purely executive one (1139b 1–3). That is why he denies the name of "προαιρεσις", "choice", to the technical or executive decision, even though this is the fruit of deliberation, if that particular thing for the sake of which this decision is being made is not *itself* decided upon by deliberation.

To return to the weak, calculating, uncontrolled man, who disapproves of adultery but is tempted about his neighbour's wife: he gives way to the temptation and sets out to seduce her; then he calculates how best to do this and shows plenty of cleverness in his calculations. If he had been a licentious man, an ακολαστος, the decision to seduce her would have been a 'choice', and the volition to perform each of the steps that he reckoned would enable him to succeed would in turn each have been a 'choice' too. For the decision to seduce this woman was simply the particular application of his general policy of pursuing sensual enjoyment. But although the uncontrolled man perhaps reckons how to proceed—once he has given way to the temptation to go after this woman—in exactly the same way as the licentious man, his volitions in performing the steps that he calculates will enable him to succeed are not 'choices'. (Aristotle, of course, does not set up a word for 'volition' as I have been using it.) So we have to say that the uncontrolled man carries out a deliberation how to execute what would have been a 'choice' if he had been an ἀκόλαστος; this, however, is something for which Aristotle has no regular name—for he has no general use of a psychological verb or abstract noun corresponding to "ἑκούσιον" (usually translated "voluntary") as "προαιρεῖσθαι" ("choose"), "προαίρεσις" ("choice"), correspond to "προαιρετον" ("chosen"). Of course he regards the uncontrolled man as acting voluntarily. When he describes this man as calculating cleverly, he says he will get what he 'proposes' (προτίθεται); and this verb expresses a volition, or perhaps rather an intention. Aristotle ought, we may say, to have seen that he was here employing a key concept in the theory of action, but he did not do so; the innocent unnoticeable verb he uses receives no attention from him.

Let us return to the point that a technical 'choice' is never the only 'choice' that is made by the man who makes it. The definition of 'choice' as ὄρεξις βουλευτική—deliberative wanting—would not at first sight seem to justify this. The calculating uncontrolled man choosing means of seduction—he wants them, surely, i.e. has an ὄρεξις for them, and this is a result of deliberation. However, there is—what may give us pause in making this criticism—a puzzling remark in that passage in Book VI (1139a 17–b 13) where Aristotle devotes most discussion to this definition of 'choice'. He says "... choice does not exist without intellect and judgment, *nor yet without* moral character." ... οὔτ' ἄνευ νου και διανοιας οὔτ' ἄνευ ἠθικης ἐστιν ἑξεως ἡ προαιρεσις. That sentence, in fact, starts with the word "διο"—"That is why". It is puzzling, because while the previous sentences give ample grounds for saying that choice involves intelligence, they don't seem to give any ground for saying that it involves moral character. However, the succeeding sentence starts "For"—so perhaps we should look for the explanation there first. "For doing well, and its opposite, does not exist without judgment and character." εὐπραξια γαρ και το ἐναντιον ἐν πραξει ἄνευ διανοιας και ἠθους οὐκ ἐστιν. That does not seem to help us much. A little farther on, however, he tells us "The end, absolutely speaking, is not anything one *makes*, but something one *does*. For doing well is the end, and that is the object of the wanting (ἡ δ'ὄρεξις τουτου). That is why choice is appetitive (ὀρεκτικη) intelligence or intelligent wanting."

This brings us back to our first defence; namely, that something is only a 'choice' if it is of means to the objects of a man's 'will' (βούλησις); hence, however much calculation may have gone into determining it, if it is of what is only a means to the objects of a man's ἐπιθυμίαι, his 'desires', then unless his 'will' in life *is* to satisfy these desires (as holds of the licentious man) it is not a 'choice'. Thus the second defence resolves into the first. The second defence was that since some deliberation is done with a view to executing a 'choice', something may be reached as a result of deliberation even when the significant decision what to do has already been made; and if this has *not* been made by deliberation (κριθεν ἐκ της βουλης), then it was not a 'choice', and the results of deliberations how to execute it won't be 'choices' either. Well, the question whether the significant decision is reached by deliberation seems to reduce to the question whether it is made with a view to the objects of the man's 'will' (βούλησις). Now our question about this was: what does Aristotle suppose 'will' (βούλησις) to be? Why, we asked, shouldn't we say that the uncontrolled man has a 'will' for the pleasure he hopes to obtain from seducing his neighbour's wife? The answer we get suggested by the passage in Book VI is: the uncontrolled man is not prepared to say: "This is my idea of good work (ἐυπραξια), this is the kind of life I want." Whereas, of course, that is the attitude of the licentious man, the ἀκολαστος: a life spent doing such things is his idea of a well-spent life—and a fig for moral virtue. It is not that the licentious man thinks licentiousness is moral virtue; what he thinks is rather that this is a good way to carry on. "One should pursue the present pleasure", δει το παρον ἡδυ διωκειν, doesn't mean: it's virtuous, or morally obligatory, to do that—but: that's the thing to do!

Now, why can't one have 'choice' without moral character of some sort? I think Aristotle does not explain this, beyond saying that 'doing well', 'a good way of carrying on' is the end of any 'choice'; i.e. any sort of decision which does not have in view what one thinks of as a good way of proceeding in one's life, does *not* qualify to be a 'choice'.

His thesis, then, clearly is that there is no such thing as your acting with ἐυπραξια, 'doing well', in view unless you have some sort of moral character, virtuous or vicious. Now, how is this? Let us imagine some cases.

Someone thinks that it is a good sort of life always to get the better of people by tricking them, taking them in, defrauding them; to do that is to be strong and not soft and not a sucker oneself, and to get the best of whatever's going; whereas the honest man is weak and soft and a fool, and always gets the worst of things. A particular decision to cheat X will be a 'choice' of something here and now which he makes for the sake of doing well as he conceives it.

Another case: Someone thinks that he will do well if he spends his life in scientific research; to do this he must have leisure; to get the money for his living expenses he does a disgraceful but not time-consuming thing: one great fraud.

These are two rather different types of case; however, in both of them it would be natural enough to say that the man is described as having a sort of moral character. On Aristotle's view, a character exists only when there is an habitual performance of the typical acts of that character. Now I have described the cases so that the men's ends are clear, but I have put in only one act for each. The first case is not credibly described on the supposition that there is only one such act. This one act with a view to this sort of 'doing well'—what is supposed to have preceded it? Has he done things of the same sort, but not done them under any such conception? under what conception, then?—say in obedience to a mentor, or attracted by the particular gains of each action? Very well; but what is to make us call this the first act done with a view to that sort of 'doing well'? It is not enough for the agent to have those thoughts; suppose he had them on just one occasion—that would not show that he was acting so as to 'do well' in that kind of way, only that he had indulged in a certain picture of his actions. Only if they are the thoughts which come to habitually inspire those actions shall we be able to say: that is his end, that is his idea of a good way of going on. If, on the other hand, he had not done any actions of the sort before, then still more one would want plenty of actions performed under the influence of his new thoughts before one could recognise one as done with a view to this sort of 'doing well' rather than as, say, an experiment in wrongdoing.

The other case is different; here the single act which is to be the object of a choice is not the kind of act which the agent supposes to be the way to spend his life well. If the agent had never done any scientific research or study at all, then the description of the case would be suspect. Either it would be nonsense, or it would be a description of someone under a fantastic illusion. Perhaps it is possible to conceive something as the activity you aim to spend your life at even though you never do it at all, even in a feeble and elementary fashion. But then either it would have to be something you could understand without doing it (like riding horses, say), or you could only want the name, no doubt with some piece of imagination attached—as if, e.g., someone who had never learnt any mathematics wanted to become a mathematician because of the expression on the face of a mathematician he knew, and had no other conception of a good way of spending his life: that was it, for him. This would rather be a lunatic obsession than a conception of a certain sort of doing well as the end.

If, then, 'choice' is only of those things which are done as means to 'doing well', we may concede that Aristotle is right in saying that it does not occur without moral character, i.e. without good or bad habitual action. But there is no reason to say that the action which is the subject of 'choice' must itself be the act of a virtue or a vice. That will only be so where the objects of 'choice' are (in Greenwood's phrase) constitutive means towards the (putative) good way of going on. In the second case I described, the fraudulent act was a productive means; and if the man did not perform other fraudulent acts, this act would not mean that he was a fraudulent man—i.e. that he had the vice of being fraudulent.

The notion of 'choice' as conceived by Aristotle, his προαιρεσις, is a very peculiar one. I used to think it spurious. If it had been a winner, like some other Aristotelian concepts, would not "pro-heretic" be a word as familiar to us as "practical" is?

At any rate, 'choice' cannot do all the work Aristotle wants to make it do. The uncontrolled man who has further intentions in doing what he does, whose actions are deliberate, although the deliberation is in the interests of a desire which conflicts with what he regards as doing well—to describe his action we need a concept (our 'intention') having to do with will or appetition: not just ἐπιθυμια, 'desire', for that may be only a feeling.

Aristotle talks as if 'desire' were a force (1147a 34), but this is only a metaphor. He will have it that if one acts against one's convictions, one's judgment has always failed in some way under the influence of 'desire' or some other passion. One fails to know or remember either the last premise or, possibly, the conclusion. There are such cases. For example, a man who disapproves of adultery may fail to find out something which he easily could have found out, and so may commit adultery through culpable ignorance of a particular premise: "This woman, whom I have picked up at a party, is someone's wife"—his failure to find out being explained by his passion. And similarly for failure to get or keep clear before one's mind already known facts, with their implications for action in view of one's ends; and for lies one may tell inwardly or outwardly when one wants to do wrong. But Aristotle writes as if these were the only cases of doing what you believe is wrong. He apparently cannot admit the case where a person forms a perfectly clear-headed intention of acting contrary to his convictions. On one interpretation the trouble always concerns one of the particular premises; on another, Aristotle allows a case where the sinner is clear about all these, but then fails to draw the conclusion; at most he draws it verbally, without knowledge of what he is saying.

The usual explanations of this are that Aristotle was a Greek, that he was still under Plato's influence, etc. No doubt there is something in that; particularly when he restricts the explanation "he repeats the thing, but it's just babble like a drunk man reciting Empedocles" to the particular premise: or possibly to that and the conclusion. It is, surely, an explanation far better suited to enunciation of the universal premise, say: "No one should commit adultery" or "It is disgraceful to get very drunk", by the man who is about to do it. Aristotle explicitly wants to exempt the universal sort of knowledge from 'being dragged about like a slave'.

However, I suspect that he was also influenced by his own conception of practical reasoning. To set out the form of practical reasoning is to set out the form of deliberation (βουλευσις). If it is all made explicit (as of course it hardly would be in real life, since one does not need to advert to the obvious) its formal character becomes quite clear. You have a set of premises starting with a universal one to the effect that a kind of thing A is, say, profitable for a kind of being B, and proceeding through intermediate premises like "C's are A's" and "a C can be obtained by a procedure D" and "a procedure D can be carried out by doing E", together with another premise to the effect that you are, or someone whose profit is your concern is, a B; and if the action E is something that you can do, then it is clear that the conclusion of this reasoning is for you to do E. But let us consider what this means. Does it mean that if you have embarked on the reasoning you *must* do E? Aristotle seems to have thought so. At least he thought you must do E unless something prevented you—the something might be the drive of 'desire', ἐπιθυμια, *against* doing E. When making this point, he often gave examples of practical syllogisms in which there is a certain necessity about the conclusion.—"It is necessary to taste everything sweet, and this is sweet" (1147a 29); "Every man must walk, and I am a man"; "Now no man must walk, and I am a man". The last two examples come from the *Movement of Animals*, Chapter VII. The man does the thing in question (walks or halts) at once, if not prevented from walking in the one case, or forced to walk in the other. There are two features suggesting the necessity of the conclusion—the gerundive form, and the type of universality in the premise.

> Every man has got to walk
> I am a man
> I have got to walk

is a formally valid deductive argument—I will call such an argument a proof-syllogism. I mean that it is a proof of the conclusion, if only the premises are true. Now Aristotle had special ideas about proof, so he would not have agreed to say what I have just said. "Every man has got to walk" is not a changeless truth, so he would have said this is not apodeictic (see, e.g., 1040a 33–5). Disregarding this let us merely note the formal validity of the reasoning as a deduction. Further, let us grant that if I agree to the premises and therefore to the conclusion, and say "I have got to walk", speaking quite seriously, it would be queer of me not to walk, if nothing prevented me.

Now let us look at another example:

> I need a covering,
> A cloak is a covering,
> I need a cloak;
> I must make what I need,
> I need a cloak,
> I must make a cloak.

The conclusion, that a cloak must be made, Aristotle says, *is* an action: τo συμπερασμα τo ἱματιον ποιητεον πραξις ἐστι. So here is a 'choice'. But, he goes on, action has a starting point—and so he sketches the reasoning with a view to execution of the 'choice': "If there's to be a cloak, first such and such is needed, and if such and such, so and so", εἰ ἱματιον ἐσται, ἀναγκη τοδε πρωτον, εἰ δε τοδε, τοδε and this last the man does at once. Now it is hard to tell whether Aristotle reflected that "I need a cloak" is not a formally valid deductive conclusion from "I need a covering and a cloak is a covering". The fact that it is not, is, I should contend, no criticism of the syllogism as a piece of practical reasoning. But it is possible that if he had been challenged about this, he would have said one could amend the syllogism by putting in that a cloak was the best covering or the easiest to make or something of that sort. (Cf. *Nicomachean Ethics* 1112b 16.) For he is marked by an anxiety to make practical reasoning out to be as like as possible to speculative reasoning. "They work just the same", he says in the *Movement of Animals*, ἐοικε παραπλησιως συμβαινειν, and seems to be referring to a necessitation of the conclusion. But you do not get this where various ways of obtaining the end are possible.

A further sign is that when he is looking at practical syllogism in this light—as necessarily yielding the conclusion—his examples of the first universal premises always go "It's needed", "It's expedient", "such and such a kind of being ought to do such and such a kind of thing". He wants a "must" in the conclusion in the verbalised form in which he gives it in the *Movement of Animals*, though each time he gives the conclusion he adds —"and that's an action". But when he is not talking about this automatic-machine aspect of the practical syllogism—which he is keen on because he thinks it helps to make it clear how the syllogism κινει, how it sets the human animal in motion—then we have such a universal premise as "Heavy waters are unwholesome". Here the *De Anima* formulation (of a doctrine also expressed in the *Nicomachean Ethics* at 1040b 16, though not so clearly) that the starting-point of the whole business is what you want (the ἀρχη is the ὀρεκτον) can come into play. And we may remark that there are two possible conclusions of the reasoning about heavy waters, according as you want to be healthy or not. That, of course, sounds absurd; but let the universal be "Strong alkalis are deadly poison", and it is easy to spell out the practical reasoning of the suicide. Aristotle recognises this two-way possibility at *Metaphysics* IX, 1046b 5–7.

It looks as if, in his enthusiasm for making practical reasoning like theoretical and explaining its power to set one in motion (aided, no doubt, by his own picture of proof and by the Platonic conception of sin as error, which he did not entirely shake off), Aristotle did not notice some significant features of his discovery; the fact that though it is perfectly correct to call practical reasoning "reasoning", and though some practical syllogisms are also (in my sense) proof syllogisms, i.e. are entailments, in general practical syllogisms have a different form from proof syllogisms.

Consider:

Owning a Launderette would make me wealthy.
There is scope for opening a Launderette on such-and-such premises

and so on down to where I might get going. This is practical reasoning, and given all the premises it is a formal matter what the conclusion is, in the form 'so I'll . . .'. Whether, if it is I who have put out the syllogism, I *draw* the conclusion, depends on whether I actively want to be wealthy and am working out this one of the many possibilities with a view to action—I might be doing it idly, or as an academic example. If by a practical syllogism you mean—as Aristotle did (*De Anima* 433 a 15)—one that terminates in action, and the purpose of which is to act, then this won't be practical; but if you mean a *type* of reasoning—i.e. reasoning reaching from a general sort of objective to something one can choose to do here and now—then it will be practical (St. Thomas would call it "theoretical *de practicis*" (*Summa Theologica* I Q. 14 art. 16c.). In general, people would not trouble to work such things out except with a view to action.

We have seen two strands in Aristotle's thought. First there is the explanation of how the human being is set in motion by thought, and second there is the idea of the thing wanted as the starting-point for such thought. For the first he seems to have wanted, not only a necessity in the connections which is not always present in practical reasonings, but also a compulsiveness about the universal premise, a 'must' about it: that is, it seems he wanted a universal premise acceptance of which implies intellectual acknowledgment of it as the guide to action. The need for necessity in the connections can fairly be discounted. Then we can happily combine the two strands by postulating at the back of all these premises a first premise to the effect that only such-and-such is doing well, is happiness or blessedness, 'the good for man'. Aristotle's grand universal premise is that blessedness is activity in accordance with virtue, especially intellectual virtue. The argument for this as the true premise is the *Nicomachean Ethics* itself. If the truth of this premise is acknowledged, then it is itself acknowledged as the ultimate guide to action. For blessedness, or doing well, is the end that anyone must have so far as he has a rational end, that is to say so far as he has 'will', i.e. the kind of wanting that belongs in the rational part, at all. (Cf. *De Anima* 432b 5–7.)

Here we touch on the difference between Aristotle and Hume. Hume's doctrine that reason is inert, that for considerations to lead to any action a sentiment, a passion, is required may be compared to Aristotle's "It is not reason as such that sets in motion; but reason which is with a view to something and is practical" (1139a 36). Aristotle's 'will' will then be a 'calm passion' in Hume's terminology. But they disagree about the applicability of the descriptions "in accordance with reason" and "not in accordance with reason" to actions and wants.

I suggest that the idea of rational wanting should be explained in terms of what is wanted being wanted *qua* conducive to or part of 'doing well', or blessedness. If one admits that what one wants is no good, but still one wants it, it is, in Aristotle's conception, merely the object of a passion; when the thing that one so wants is a pleasure, though it is no good (like smoking in some people's view) then one is being led simply by 'desire', ἐπιθυμια. For though what constitutes blessedness is necessarily utterly pleasant, it is not something one wants because it is a pleasure even though it should be no good; on the contrary, it is the object of will as the best possible thing for a human being, being the activity of his rational part and the activity that is an end, not a means.

For as seeing can be seen to be what the eye is for, so under-standing—the enjoyment of the truth—can be seen to be what the mind is for. But here we must note a certain split in Aristotle's thought. For the highest blessedness he thought of as something divine, which we should grasp at to the poor extent that we can—taking the side of and imitating the immortal. He coins a word for what we should do, namely "to immortalize" (ἀθανατιζειν 1177b 33), sounding like an echo of "to Medize" which means to be on the side of and imitate the Persian. But he acknowledges that in the ordinary course of life for most people 'doing well' amounts to something more mundane: a successful and honourable conduct of life, the heart of which is, if one judges rightly, action in accordance with *moral* virtue.

Apart from being ruled by passion (this is what I want, even if it is no good) 'doing well' is what anyone wants in some obscure and indeterminate way. One could call it that part of blessedness for which one's own action is essential. Aristotle's unrealistic conception of the clearcutness of people's ends seems on investigation not to be so bad as it looked. For the many objectives that are no good are allowed for in his thought. The assumption of clearcutness is the assumption that people generally know what they count as 'doing well'—i.e. that they definitely so count being rich or being famous or the life of knowledge.

My eventual goal has been to expound the concept of 'practical truth' and the discussion of *Nicomachean Ethics* Book VI, Chapter II on 'choice'. I will start from 1139a 21. "What affirmation and negation are in judgment, pursuit and avoidance are in desire." That is, one can say "yes" or "no" both to a statement and to a proposal. Suppose, then, that the statement should say that doing such and such is 'doing well'. There is the "yes" in judgment and the "yes" in the will, meaning that one wants to do that sort of thing. For to characterise it as 'doing well' is *eo ipso* to propose it as an object of 'will'—to put it up as a candidate for 'will', βουλησις.

"So," Aristotle goes on, "since moral virtue is a disposition of one's choice, while choice is deliberated wanting, these things show that the judgment must be true and the wanting right, if the choice is to be sound, and the one must say and the other pursue the same thing." We may remark that the one must say and the other pursue the same thing if there is to be any 'choice' at all, sound or unsound. So far we have only mentioned the judgment on what εὐπραξια, doing well, is. A false judgment on this necessarily means that if there is a 'choice' at all the wanting in it is wrong. To make this clear, imagine a worldling's idea of doing well. If the worldly man has any wants that are right, they don't occur in his 'choices'. Any 'choice' that he makes, since in 'choice' the wanting goes after what the judgment declares to be doing well, must involve wrong wanting.

Can the judgment be false at a lower level than one's idea of doing well, without the wanting being wrong if they are in accord? Suppose the man has judged truly, as Aristotle would say and as I want to say, that to act justly is necessary for doing well, but falsely that justice would be done by dividing all the goods available in the country into equal shares according to the number of the population and assigning each share to one person by picking name and number of share out of a hat; or that it is justice for a poor man to be punished for assaulting a rich one, but not vice versa. I am not speaking of particular procedures, but of judgments about what *sort* of procedures are just.

It appears to me that only when we get to questions where it is difficult to know the truth, or questions as to facts which the agent can't be expected to have found out, is there any chance for the wanting of what is judged a means to doing well to be right when the judgment itself is wrong. This then will be why Aristotle said in Book III (1110b 31) that ignorance in choice, ἡ ἐν τῇ προαιρεσει ἀγνοια, is the cause not of involuntariness but of scoundrelism. He himself laid down the rule about difficulty at 1113b 33–1114a 2.

We now approach the great question: what does Aristotle mean by "practical truth"? He calls it the good working, or the work, of practical judgment; and practical judgment is judgment of the kind described, terminating in action. It is practical truth when the judgments involved in the formation of the 'choice' leading to the action are all true; but the practical truth is not the truth of those *judgments*. For it is clearly that 'truth in agreement with right desire', ἀληθεια ὁμολογως ἐχουσα τῇ ὀρεξει τῇ ὀρθῇ (1139a 30), which is spoken of as the good working (εὖ), or the work (ἐργον), of practical intelligence. That is brought about—i.e. made true—by action (since the description of what he does is made true by his doing it), provided that a man forms and executes a good 'choice'. The man who forms and executes an evil 'choice' will also make true *some* description of what he does. He will secure, say, if he is competent, that such and such a man has his eyes put out or his hands cut off, that being his judgment of what it is just to do. But his description "justice performed" of what he has done will be a lie. He, then, will have produced practical falsehood.

"Since everything that is done about them is false, how should these be gods?"—The notion of *truth or falsehood in action* would quite generally be countered by the objection that "true" and "false" are senseless predicates as applied to what is done. If I am right there is philosophy to the contrary in Aristotle. And if, as I should maintain, the idea of the *description under which* what is done is done is integral to the notion of action, then these predicates apply to actions strictly and properly, and not merely by an extension and in a way that ought to be explained away.

ARISTOTLE ON JUSTICE:
A PARADIGM OF PHILOSOPHY
Renford Bambrough

AT the beginning of Book V of the *Nicomachean Ethics* Aristotle distinguishes between two senses of the word δικαιοσύνη or "justice". There is one sense of the word in which justice is equivalent to the whole of moral virtue, and in which the just man is the righteous man, the man who is upright and honourable and virtuous in general. There is another sense of the word in which justice is one of the particular or specific virtues, side by side with courage and temperance and generosity. It is the virtue whose field of application is our dealings with other human beings in matters of property, contract, and so on. A man who is just in the first sense will necessarily be just in the second sense, but a man may be just in the second sense without being just in the first sense. A businessman may be scrupulously honest in all his commercial dealings, and may nevertheless be a libertine, a coward, a miser, a man full of envy, malice, and all uncharitableness.

The point that Aristotle is making in this passage can be better presented in English by expressing it in terms of the concept of *honesty* rather than the concept of justice. The wider use of the word "just" is obsolescent, but we can still speak of an honest man either in the narrower sense of a man who does not steal or commit fraudulent conversion, or in the wider sense of a man who (to use other expressions that still, in modern English, have the same duality in their use) is a man of complete *integrity*, who is *fair* in all his *dealings*. Although Aristotle, here as often, explicitly discusses the use of ordinary Greek words and phrases, it is clear that he is concerned with substantive and important questions about the relations between moral virtues, and not with linguistic facts for their own sake. His discussion of justice is akin, both in its texture and in its outcome, to Wollaston's efforts to reduce all the virtues to truth-telling, or, as Professor D. M. MacKinnon puts it in his excellent short discussion of Wollaston in *A Study in Ethical Theory* (Black, 1957) to present all vices as forms of *cheating.*

Aristotle is well aware, although he does not put the points in exactly these terms, that his discussion of the two kinds of justice gives rise to the following questions:

(1) If justice in the first sense is equivalent to the whole of moral virtue, why do we refer to it by means of two different expressions, sometimes calling it justice and sometimes calling it the whole of moral virtue?

(2) If justice in the first sense is something different from justice in the second sense, why do we use the same word to refer to both?

The innuendo behind these two questions is that we might as well dispense with the first use of the word "justice" altogether. It is either redundant or worse than redundant. It can cause nothing but confusion, since it refers to something for which we already have another name, and since the word is in any case pre-empted for a use in which it refers to something different from justice-in-general and virtue-in-general, namely the particular virtue of justice. The fact that Aristotle has to take the trouble to explain these points might itself be taken as an indication that the ordinary Greek usage of these expressions is confused and in need of revision.

If we look more closely at Aristotle's account of the concept of justice, we can see in it an implicit answer to this complaint. In the first place he explains that although justice in the first sense is equivalent to the whole of moral virtue, it is nevertheless not identical with the whole of moral virtue, for it differs from it in its essence (εἶναι). It is fortunately unnecessary to explain here in general terms what Aristotle means by a difference in εἶναι; his remarks about the difference between general justice and the whole of moral virtue are clear in spite of the obscurity of that particular term. When we speak of moral virtue we have in mind the excellence of the individual human being, considered *statically,* as an attribute, as the nature or quality of the man who is said to be virtuous. When we speak of justice in the first sense we have in mind the *functioning* of that excellence in the individual man's relationships with other men. We are still speaking of the same excellence, but we are now considering it *dynamically*, as a capacity or power which the virtuous or just man exercises in his dealings with others, not only in the restricted field in which the specific virtue of justice operates, but over the whole range of the man's dealings with other men.

In other words, there is an important distinction between justice in the first sense and moral virtue in general, which is marked by using different words for the two concepts. Although they are connected, and although the connection between them is important, and must be pointed out by the moral philosopher, both because it is important and because it is hidden by the use of two different expressions for the two connected concepts, they nevertheless *are* two different concepts; they are distinguishable in such a way as to explain and justify the ordinary use of two different expressions to refer to them.

Secondly, and similarly, although justice in the first sense is distinct from justice in the second sense, it is nevertheless fundamentally connected with it. The range of justice in the first sense is as wide as the range of virtue in general, while justice in the second sense, like any other particular virtue, has its own specific field of application. But justice in the first sense is connected with justice in the second sense by the fact that they both concern our relations with other human beings, and it is this connection that we mark by using the same word for both concepts. Although they are distinct, and although the distinction between them is important, and must be pointed out by the moral philosopher, both because it is important and because it is hidden by the use of the same word for the two distinct concepts, they nevertheless *are* two connected concepts; they are connected in such a way as to explain and justify the ordinary use of one and the same word to refer to both of them.

Another way of trying to express the difference and the connection between justice in general and moral virtue in general would be to say that they are two *aspects* of the same thing: but this way of speaking is likely to be obscure to anybody who has not already seen the connection and the difference, while anybody who has already seen the connection and the difference does not need to speak in this way.

It can now be made clear that the revisions of ordinary language suggested by the questions of Aristotle's imaginary opponent would not achieve their purpose. If we had only one word for virtue in general, it would be necessary for moral philosophers to point out that there was a distinction between virtue in general and justice in the first sense, that is to say, between the whole of moral virtue considered statically and the whole of moral virtue considered dynamically, which was hidden by ordinary language. But such philosophers would have to recognise that the language as they found it marked a connection which was not explicitly marked in the language in which they made their philosophical point. Similarly, if we had two different words for the two different senses of justice, it would be necessary for moral philosophers to point out that there was a connection between the concepts referred to by these two words, although the connection would then be hidden by ordinary language. And such philosophers would have to recognise that the language as they found it marked a distinction that was not explicitly marked in the language in which they made their philosophical point.

All this is important for the understanding of Book V of the *Nicomachean Ethics*, which is in turn important for the understanding of Aristotle's moral and general philosophy. But it has an even wider importance, and it is with this wider importance that I am here concerned. I suggest that Aristotle's discussion of the two senses of the word δικαιοσύνη is not only an important and interesting, but also a *typical* philosophical discussion. And I do not mean by this simply that it illustrates one particular type of philosophical discussion, in such a sense that it would be possible to give examples of other and radically different types. I mean to make the stronger claim that the main features of Aristotle's discussion of the concept of justice are the main features of philosophical discussion as such. Philosophy consists in drawing the kinds of distinctions between concepts that Aristotle draws in this passage, and in marking the kinds of connections between concepts that Aristotle marks in this passage. Good philosophy consists in exhibiting connections and distinctions which have hitherto lain hidden; in drawing distinctions without obscuring connections, and marking connections without obscuring distinctions; in exhibiting distinctions and marking connections between important and central (and therefore usually, but by no means always, very general) rather than between trivial and peripheral (and therefore usually, but not always, very specific) concepts.

I recognise that I have not so far offered any argument for my claim that this is what philosophy is, and that I have done very little even to explain what I mean by saying that this is what philosophy is. Instead of offering any such argument or explanation in explicit and general terms, I will indicate the nature of my claim, and I hope also the nature of some of my reasons for making it, by outlining its relations with a number of familiar doctrines about the nature of philosophy. My procedure will be to argue that Aristotle's discussion is a fatal counter-example to each of the theories that I shall discuss. For this purpose it is sufficient that Aristotle's discussion should be allowed to be a philosophical discussion, and unnecessary that it should be shown to be a typical or a paradigm case of a philosophical discussion.

I. PHILOSOPHY AND ORDINARY LANGUAGE

If I have given an accurate account of Aristotle's discussion of the concept of justice, and if that discussion is a typical philosophical discussion, or indeed a philosophical discussion at all, it is clear that we cannot accept either the doctrine that philosophy consists wholly in detecting and correcting departures from ordinary language or the doctrine that philosophy consists wholly in detecting and correcting deficiencies *in* ordinary language.

For (1) Aristotle shows that ordinary language obscures a distinction and a connection which a revised language could exhibit, and one such instance is sufficient to show that we shall not be able to do everything that we need to do in philosophy if we insist on the sacrosanctity of language-as-it-is; and (2) we have seen, with the help of Aristotle, that a language which revealed the distinction and the connection which ordinary language obscures would obscure the distinction and the connection which ordinary language reveals.

But a consideration of Aristotle's discussion of justice not only shows that these two accounts of the nature of philosophy are mistaken; it also shows what the motives are that might incline us to accept each of these two accounts.

163

For (3) we may be more forcibly struck by the distinction and the connection which Aristotle exhibits *in* ordinary language than by the distinction and the connection which, as he shows, are obscured by ordinary language; or (4) we may be more forcibly struck by the distinction and the connection which are obscured by ordinary language than by the distinction and the connection which, as Aristotle shows, are revealed in ordinary language.

An examination of Aristotle's remarks on the concept of justice brings to light another important point against both the accounts of the nature of philosophy that we are considering. It is inessential to the interest, the value, and the philosophical character of Aristotle's discussion that any particular one of the distinctions and connections that he is concerned with should as a matter of fact be obscured or revealed in any natural language as it is. Some philosophical discussions proceed by comparing and contrasting one natural language with another, or one part of a natural language with another part of the same natural language; others proceed by comparing and contrasting the usages of some natural language or languages with the uses of imaginary or invented languages; others again by comparing and contrasting imaginary uses of language with other imaginary uses of language. The adequate discussion of any difficult philosophical point is likely to be facilitated by a free use of all these methods, but none of them is indispensable, none of them has any general superiority to any of the others, and none of them has any general inferiority to any of the others. All that is necessary is that there should be comparison and contrast between different uses of language, each of which reveals a connection or distinction which the other obscures. And it is certain that in most cases, and probable that in all cases, each of the uses of language between which a comparison or contrast is made will *both* reveal something which the other obscures *and* obscure something which the other reveals. It is because all or most ways of marking distinctions or connections between concepts have clear advantages and clear disadvantages that philosophy is so difficult and so controversial. We shall see later that the fact that there is so much difficulty and so much controversy, that philosophical disputes have in fact been inconclusive, is not a ground for maintaining that they are necessarily or inevitably inconclusive.

II. PHILOSOPHY AS VERBAL RECOMMENDATION OR DECISION

Those who speak of philosophical theories or propositions as verbal recommendations recognise that the aim of philosophy is to reveal connections and distinctions between concepts, and they also recognise that ordinary language sometimes reveals and sometimes obscures such distinctions and connections. According to this account, the task of the philosopher is sometimes to devise forms of language which will reveal what ordinary language obscures, and sometimes to show that forms of language devised by other philosophers obscure what ordinary language or other invented uses of language can reveal. But those who give this type of account, especially when they speak of philosophical questions as requests for *decisions* about the uses of words, and of philosophical propositions as expressions of decisions on how to use words, are in danger of obscuring some important features of philosophical reflection and discussion. They give the impression that when two or more uses of language have been fully examined we are entitled to choose for ourselves which is to be accepted and which rejected.

Two misunderstandings give rise to and arise from this suggestion. In the first place, the uses of language examined or devised by philosophers are not rivals in such a sense that one is to be unconditionally preferred to others with which, in the discussion of some particular philosophical question, it has been compared and contrasted. Each of several different uses may be valuable for the light it sheds and dangerous because of the shadow it casts. Secondly, when we suggest that a particular form of words valuably reveals a certain connection or distinction, or dangerously obscures a certain connection or distinction, the question of the rightness or wrongness of the claim that we are then making is totally independent of our own wishes, preferences, or choices in the matter. Aristotle does not merely *choose to say* that justice in the first sense is distinct from and closely related to justice in the second sense and to the whole of moral virtue. He *points out* these connections and distinctions: he *shows* that they are there to be seen in the concepts that he is examining.

This point does not depend on my contention that Aristotle is right in his conclusions about the relations between the concepts of justice and virtue. If Aristotle is wrong, it is because he has overlooked something that he might have seen, or because he has claimed to see something that is not there to be seen. A philosopher who undertakes to criticise Aristotle's discussion is not entitled merely to choose to say that Aristotle's conclusions are unacceptable *to him*. He must *show what is wrong* with Aristotle's premises or arguments or observations if he is to be justified in rejecting his conclusions.

A philosophical question, like any other question, has a *right* answer, even if the right answer to a philosophical question is seldom either a plain "Yes" or a plain "No". A philosophical answer may be right, or it may be wrong, but like any other answer it will be *either* right *or* wrong.

III. PHILOSOPHY AS THE SEARCH FOR AN IDEAL LANGUAGE

Similar difficulties face another account of the nature of philosophy which is closely akin to the verbal recommendation account, namely that according to which philosophy is the attempt to construct an artificial, ideal language, a language which will mark *all* the connections and *all* the differences between concepts. This account fails to explain some of the main features of Aristotle's discussion of justice and virtue, and in fact when we try to envisage how the construction of an ideal language could help Aristotle to deal with his problem we soon see (*a*) that in any sense in which such an ideal language is possible it is also unnecessary, and (*b*) that in any sense in which such a language might be thought to be necessary it is also impossible. In the sense in which Aristotle was comparing and contrasting two languages, in one of which the two kinds of justice are referred to by the same word, and in the other of which they would be referred to by two different words, an ideal language is impossible, because no language which is a single language in this sense can *both* reveal in its idioms the close connection between the two kinds of justice *and also* reveal in its idioms the important distinction between them. On the other hand, if we count as a single language one which has separate idioms, one of which will mark the connection and the other of which will mark the distinction between the two kinds of justice, then there is no need to seek an ideal language for this purpose, since, as Aristotle shows, ordinary Greek is adequate to the task.

It is now clear that no language, natural or artificial, can be such as to dispense users of that language from the need for philosophical discussion of the kind that Aristotle provides, since (*a*) if we have a language which marks a connection and obscures a difference we shall need to have the difference pointed out to us, (*b*) if we have a language which marks a difference and obscures a connection we shall need to have the connection pointed out to us, and (*c*) if we have a language in which one idiom marks a connection and obscures a difference, and in which another idiom obscures the same connection and marks the same difference, we shall need to have it pointed out to us that the connection which one idiom marks is the connection which the other idiom obscures and that the difference which one idiom marks is the difference which the other idiom obscures.

As we have already seen, the ordinary Greek expressions for justice and moral virtue require treatment in just this last way, and it is because Aristotle so admirably provides just the kind of treatment they need that I call the beginning of Book V of the *Nicomachean Ethics* a paradigm of philosophy.

IV. PHILOSOPHY AS THE SEARCH FOR DEFINITIONS

It has often been thought that all or most philosophical problems could be solved by carefully defining the expressions around whose meaning and use the familiar controversies and perplexities of philosophy have been concentrated. This account of the nature of philosophy is closely connected with the verbal recommendation account and the ideal language account, and it shares their main defects.

A simple illustration, taken from an actual philosophical discussion in the Moral Sciences Club at Cambridge, will indicate both the plausibility and the limitations of this approach. Somebody had read a paper on "Wishing", and the discussion was largely concerned with the question "Can a wish be unconscious?" Some speakers said that consciousness was a necessary condition for being a wish, and that "unconscious wish" was a self-contradictory expression. Others replied that unconscious wishes differ from other wishes *only* in being unconscious, and that this difference is trivial as compared with the similarities. At this point a mediator interposed, impatiently: "But this is just a question of words. It all depends on what you mean by 'wish'. If we carefully define the word 'wish', we shall see at once whether or not a wish may be unconscious." Here Professor Wisdom intervened. "Tell me," he said to the mediator, "when you have defined the word 'wish', will your definition correspond to the ordinary use of the word 'wish'? If so, our problem will be left where it is, for presumably your definition will in that case preserve those features of our familiar concept of wishing which have, as we have seen, given rise to philosophical difficulty. If, on the other hand, you define the word 'wish' in some other way, you may indeed be able to say at once whether, according to your definition, a wish may be unconscious, but in that case you will not be solving *our* problem of whether a wish can be unconscious but will be solving another and simpler problem which you have chosen to express in the same form of words."

Wisdom might have put what is essentially the same point by saying that the question "What is the definition of a wish?" is one that can only be accurately answered by somebody who *already* knows whether a wish can or cannot be unconscious, and that therefore the finding of a definition cannot be a *means* to answering the question "Can a wish be unconscious?"

I think it is clear that any attempt to deal with Aristotle's questions about the concepts of justice and moral virtue by the offering of definitions would be subject to the same comments. A suggested definition will either be inaccurate, or it will preserve those features of the usage of the expressions "justice" and "moral virtue" which prompt and require the kind of discussion that Aristotle gives. In the latter case there are two possibilities: *either* (*a*) the definition will be such as to specify the connections and differences which Aristotle points out, in which case it will achieve nothing that Aristotle has not achieved without a definition; *or* (*b*) the definition will not specify those connections and differences, in which case it will not even achieve what Aristotle achieves without a definition.

The nature of Aristotle's achievement in clarifying the concept of justice, and the nature and limitations of the theories about the nature of philosophy that I have considered and rejected, and the relevance of both to the positive points about the nature of philosophy that I wish to make, can be more fully explained by

giving some account of the familiar notion of analogical predication, which Aristotle does not explicitly use in the passage on
justice, but which underlies that passage, and which is, I shall
argue, of greater philosophical importance than either Aristotle
himself or almost any of his successors has recognised.

A univocal or unambiguous predicate is one which applies in
the same sense to all the things to which it applies. For example,
all red things are red in the same sense of "red", and all square
things are square in the same sense of "square". (Of course we
may call a man a "Red" or a "square", that is to say, we may use
these terms analogically, but this complication need not concern
us here.) An equivocal expression is one which is merely ambiguous, one which is used in two totally unrelated senses. The
word "bank" may refer to the bank of a river, or to a branch of
the National Provincial Bank, and there is no connection, except
possibly a remote philological or etymological connection, between
the two uses. A case of analogical predication is one in which the
same expression is used neither univocally nor equivocally, that is
to say where the expression is not used in exactly the same way in
all the cases where it is properly used, but where the differences
between the various uses are not such as to make us say or to
justify us in saying that there is no connection between the various
uses. The term "justice" is clearly a case in point. It is *not for
nothing* that the same word is used for moral virtue in general and
for the specific virtue of justice, although these are two different
concepts. Two of Aristotle's own examples from other works will
underline the point. The verb "to be" is used analogically, as
Aristotle explains in the *Categories* and the *Metaphysics*. In the
Categories there is also some discussion of the verb "to have". I
may have a wife, a hundred pounds, four children, a headache,
an interesting past, and a problematic future.

One might say that the word "bank" as used to refer to the
bank of a river, and the word "bank" as used to refer to a branch
of the National Provincial Bank, are two different words which
happen to be spelt in the same way. Nothing would be lost by
having two different words with two different spellings for these
two different uses. And hardly anything would be gained, either,
since the uses are so far apart that consideration of the context
will nearly always prevent confusion and misunderstanding. In
the case of an analogical predicate, however, as we have seen in

discussing Aristotle's account of justice, something is gained *and* something is lost by the adoption of two words to do what is now done by the one word "justice", and something is gained and something is lost by adopting only *one* word to do what is now done by the two expressions "justice" (as used in the first sense) and "moral virtue in general".

The main defects of the various accounts of the nature of philosophy that I considered above spring from their suggestion that all terms should be univocal; that, in the old slogan, we should have one *nomen* for one *nominatum*. In particular, the definition model and the ideal language model, that is to say the models that try to link philosophy closely with the exact formal sciences, where ambiguity is anathema, try to make all philosophical terms *univocal*, on the mistaken assumption that if a term is not univocal then it will be merely *equivocal*.

I suggest that most if not all of the expressions around which philosophical debate is and always has been concentrated are neither univocal nor equivocal but *analogical*. I suggest further that what I am now putting in terms of the concept of analogy is closely connected with what Wittgenstein put in terms of his concept of family resemblances, but I will not complicate matters by going farther into that discussion here and now.

Convincing support for the suggestion that all or most philosophical disputes are concerned with analogical concepts could be provided only by a long and comprehensive survey of the main problems of philosophy. But it is possible to indicate more briefly that one very large and important class of philosophical questions, namely those concerned with the nature, scope, and limits of the concept of *knowledge*, are of the same kind as Aristotle's questions about the concept of justice, and are to be dealt with in the way in which Aristotle deals with his questions, and not in the ways suggested by the theories of the nature of philosophy to which Aristotle's discussion has proved to be a counter-example.

If we recognise that the concept of knowledge is an analogical or family resemblances concept, we can find our way out of some notorious and fundamental philosophical difficulties, and can see at the same time how we got into those difficulties in the first place.

There are two recurrent and closely connected types of philosophical doctrine which have been produced again and again by the failure of philosophers to notice that knowledge is an analogical concept, or by their failure to understand the nature and importance of analogy, and their consequent insistence that there must be an instance or type of knowledge which is the paradigm from which other instances or types regrettably decline.

These two types of doctrine are *Scepticism* and *Positivism*.

A sceptical doctrine consists in saying of some type of knowledge that it is not knowledge, and it is usually supported by pointing out that some other type of knowledge, which is alleged or allowed to be *real* knowledge, *genuine* knowledge, has a feature or features that cannot be found in the type of knowledge that is being attacked. For example: (1) The sceptic about our knowledge of the external world points out that a proposition about a material object, unlike a proposition about one's own sensations, or a proposition of formal logic or pure mathematics, is such that there is some future event or set of events, which, if it were to occur, would constitute decisive evidence against the proposition in question, and which is also such that it is logically possible that it should occur. (2) The sceptic about induction points out that any inductive argument, unlike a valid deductive argument, is such that the conjunction of its premises with the contradictory of its conclusion is not a self-contradictory proposition.

Positivism is closely akin to scepticism; in fact, it can be expressed as a more moderate and limited form of scepticism. It consists in denying the status of knowledge to some types of knowledge because they lack the characteristic features of certain other and favoured types of knowledge. For example, moral knowledge, metaphysical knowledge, and theological knowledge are said not to be *knowledge* because they have logical features which distinguish them sharply from mathematical knowledge and physical knowledge.

The main differences between positivism and scepticism are (1) that the positivist is slightly more liberal in his standards for determining what is to count as knowledge (but only *very* slightly, for he characteristically maintains that "all empirical statements are *hypotheses*"), and (2) that positivism is usually expressed in terms of the concept of meaning or of literal meaning rather than in terms of the concept of knowledge itself. But the concept of meaning, like the concepts of reason, truth, verification, proof, justification, and most if not all other epistemological concepts, is itself an analogical concept, and for the purposes of the present discussion no harm will be done by concentrating on the concept of knowledge to the neglect of these other and related analogical concepts. The positivist is *sceptical* about morality, metaphysics, and theology; he maintains that there is no *knowledge* of moral, metaphysical, and theological propositions.

The sceptic and the positivist are right in the remarks that they make about the specific differences between the various types of knowledge, and indeed their work has the great merit of increasing our awareness of the nature of the various types of knowledge and of the differences between them. But it must still be insisted that the conclusions that they draw from their observations of the various types of knowledge are fundamentally mistaken. The conclusion that those observations support is that the concept of knowledge exhibits great internal variety: that it is not the case that all knowledge is either of a single type or of a small and easily specifiable number of types, each of which has a simple and easily describable nature. We cannot *both* recognise the claims of all the types of knowledge to be types of knowledge, and the internal complexity of each separate type, *and also* cling to the assumption that it is possible and necessary to give a single, simple formula that expresses what is common and peculiar to all instances or types of knowledge and at the same time *explains* what knowledge is. The sceptic and the positivist recognise the contradiction between these two theses, but they reject the just claims of some types of knowledge to be types of knowledge instead of rejecting the false assumption from which their sceptical and positivist conclusions derive their plausibility: the false assumption that if they do not insist that the term "knowledge" is *univocal* they will be forced to admit that it is *merely equivocal*.

The arguments of moral sceptics illustrate in a particularly striking way the sources and the limitations of this line of reasoning. It has repeatedly been maintained that there is no such thing as moral knowledge, and this contention has been supported by pointing out the differences between morality on the one hand and mathematics and science on the other. But however important the differences may be between moral knowledge and mathematical knowledge, or between moral knowledge and scientific knowledge, *they are no more important than the differences between mathematical knowledge and scientific knowledge*. The positivist, and other moral sceptics who attack moral knowledge while defending mathematical and scientific knowledge, are therefore being inconsistent, since they attach more importance to some of the internal boundaries of the concept of knowledge than they do to others, although they not only do not show, but could not show, that the differences to which they attach greater importance are in fact greater or more important.

The connection of Aristotle's doctrine of analogy with Wittgenstein's concept of family resemblances may be illustrated by considering a simple non-philosophical example. Let us imagine that we are trying to communicate to a visitor from Mars an understanding of our language and some of our institutions and ways of life. Perhaps he has never encountered anything in the nature of a *competition* before. He therefore has great difficulty in understanding what it is to *win* a game, a battle, a war, or an election. We might begin by taking him to Newmarket and telling him that the horse that reaches the post first has won the race. If we then take him to the White City and show him a runner reaching the tape first, he may quickly see the parallel between the two cases, so that we should need to spend very little time at Brands Hatch or at the Wembley Pool. If we then take him to Wimbledon or Lord's he is likely to be in great difficulties, and to fail to see any connection between the earlier examples and the later. When we have finally made him understand that in tennis and cricket, as well as in racing, there is such a thing as *winning*, our difficulties will not be over. We may take him to the House of Commons, where the Government has just won a vote of confidence, or to the Law Courts, where a defendant or a barrister has just won his case. We shall also have to present him with examples of people winning spot prizes at dances, *slow* bicycle races, beauty contests, prizes at flower shows, golden opinions, fame and renown. He will perhaps complain that he sees nothing in common between winning a bet and winning a by-election.

We know, because we know what winning is and what competition is, that all these multifarious examples are related to each other in such a way as to justify us in calling them all cases of winning. His difficulties will arise from the fact that there is no obvious common element between all the various cases, and that there is no way of saying what all the cases of winning have in common, except by saying that they are cases of winning or by saying something equally trivial.

The concept of winning, like the concept of knowledge, has such great internal variety, covers such a manifold of apparently unrelated examples, that in the case of either concept an adequate understanding can be given only by presenting a wide range of examples and comparing and contrasting them. If our Martian visitor refused to believe that anything could be a case of winning unless it conformed closely to the cases in which a man or a car or a horse reaches a winning-post first, he would be in the position of the sceptic who refuses to allow that anything can count as knowledge unless it is mathematical or has the same degree of formality as mathematics. If he was prepared to add other games but not prepared to add elections, wars, and court cases, he would be in the position of the positivist who has two paradigms instead of one, but who is as reluctant to go beyond his two paradigms as the sceptic is to go beyond his single paradigm.

In the 24th chapter of Book I of the *Posterior Analytics* Aristotle remarks that a word may have *one meaning* without necessarily referring to *one thing*. To give a clear, accurate, and useful account of justice or goodness or beauty, or of meaning, reason, proof, truth, or necessity, or of matter or man or mind, is to walk the tight-rope between denying the unity of the meaning and denying the manifold variety of the instances. It is because Aristotle and Wittgenstein could look to right and to left at the same time without succumbing to metaphysical double vision that they are the two most successful equilibrists in the history of philosophy.

INDEX

Hintikka, J., 75
Hippocratic writings, 48ff
Hirst, R. J., 125
homonymy, 72f, 95
honesty, 159
Hume, D., 155
hypotheses, Plato's meaning, 23
—use by mathematicians, 21ff

individuality, basis of, 102f
"is", existential and predicative uses, 8, 29
Isocrates, 42, 43, 46, 49, 58

justice, two senses, 159

Kant, I., 78, 107, 118
Kapp, E., 68n
kind-ladders, 61, 63ff
Kneale, W. and M., 85, 88
knowledge, empirical, 18
—moral, 172
—of objects and of propositions, 23
—theory of, 118

language, ideal, philosophy as search for, 166f
—ordinary, and philosophy, 163ff
Le Blond, J. M., 104
Lee, H. D. P., 68n
Locke, John, 114, 116
logic, and language, 25
—philosophy of, 99, 117
logos, in Aristotle, 73

MacKinnon, D. M., 160
many questions, fallacy of, 68
Megarians, 45
metaphysics, and logic, 32
Moore, G. E., 86, 99, 112, 113, 117n
moral virtue, and justice, 160ff
Moreau, J., 2n
Murphy, N. R., 2n, 9n, 11n

non-contradiction, principle of, 15, 60

ontological enquiry, 99f
Orr, S. S., 2n
Owen, G. E. L., 2n, 15n

paraphrase, overworked, 80, 81, 88
philosophical discussion, nature of, 162f
philosophy, Aristotle's meaning, 58
Plato, and dialectic, 54ff
Platonic Definitions, 62
Popper, K. R., 34
positivism, 171

predication, analogical, 169
Protagoras, 39, 45ff, 50

Quine, W. V., 74, 80n, 110

real, and existent, 92
—Plato's use of, 4ff
—and true, relation, 2f
—as value-predicate, 7
recommendations, verbal, 165
reductio ad absurdum, 45
Rhetoric, Arts of, 39
Robinson, R., 19n, 68n
Ross, W. D., 15n, 70, 76n, 123, 139
Russell, B., 99
Ryan, Columba, 103n
Ryle, G., vii, 123, 125ff, 133f

scepticism, 171
self-existence, 116f
Sextus Empiricus, 44
Shorey, P., 13n
Simon, 49
Socrates, and eristic, 50ff
sorts, and things, 107f
Speusippus, 62, 74n
steresis, 105
Strawson, P. F., 29, 74, 118n
substance, primary and secondary, 101f
substantive-hungry words, 94
Suidas, 45
syllogisms, practical and proof, 154

theology, Christian, 115
—and ontology, in Aristotle, 111f
Theophrastus, 62
"thing", meaning, 101
Thompson, E. S., 12n
truths, synthetic a priori, 33
Turnbull, R. G., 13n

universals and particulars, differences, 19

Vendler, Z., 135f
verbs, in present and perfect, 122ff
Vlastos, G., 19n, 36n

Wedberg, A., 19n
White, M., 80n
winning, concept of, 173f
Wisdom, J., 168
Wittgenstein, L., 67, 79, 170, 173
Wollaston, W., 160

Xenocrates, 43, 49, 62
Xenophon, 52

Zeno, 44f